A Path

Through Jesus

BY

Frances Munro

Trafford
PUBLISHING

Previous Book by the same author;

FOOTSTEPS OF MY SOUL

Published by Trafford Publishing in 2006

Order this book online at www.trafford.com/07-1558
or email orders@trafford.com

Most Trafford titles are also available at major online book retailers.

Note for Librarians: A cataloguing record for this book is available from Library
and Archives Canada at www.collectionscanada.ca/amicus/index-e.html

Printed in Victoria, BC, Canada.

ISBN: 978-1-4251-3882-0

*We at Trafford believe that it is the responsibility of us all, as both individuals
and corporations, to make choices that are environmentally and socially sound.
You, in turn, are supporting this responsible conduct each time you purchase a
Trafford book, or make use of our publishing services. To find out how you are
helping, please visit www.trafford.com/responsiblepublishing.html*

*Our mission is to efficiently provide the world's finest, most comprehensive
book publishing service, enabling every author to experience success.
To find out how to publish your book, your way, and have it available
worldwide, visit us online at www.trafford.com/10510*

 www.trafford.com

North America & international
toll-free: 1 888 232 4444 (USA & Canada)
phone: 250 383 6864 ♦ fax: 250 383 6804 ♦ email: info@trafford.com

The United Kingdom & Europe
phone: +44 (0)1865 722 113 ♦ local rate: 0845 230 9601
facsimile: +44 (0)1865 722 868 ♦ email: info.uk@trafford.com

10 9 8 7 6 5 4 3 2

Self Help Guide and Formula to Life

Index

D

E

F

G

H

I

J

K

L

M

N

O

P

Q

R

S

T

U

V

W

Y

Z

Foreword
by
Michael Munro

I feel very privileged to be able to make a contribution to this book. This is like nothing that I have read previously, in as much that many of the beliefs that I have established and become comfortable with over my life have been laid open to question.

Beliefs of any sort, not just religious, are things that we can ground with because we think that they are laid in fact, and we can always rely on them to be there for us when we need them. They give us stability and a reference point when we come under pressure in some way during our daily lives. They don't always come from within. Some are taught or inherited, which again gives them an implied reliability and truth, but this can also be incorrect.

The problems start to come when some of these well established values come under scrutiny and can be questioned; this is something that I have experienced to an extent from reading this book.

Of course not all my beliefs have been destroyed – far from it, there are only a few in the many that I have had to review. In many cases they have been reinforced, which made me feel really good and righteous as someone far more knowledgeable, powerful and ethereal was telling me that I had been right all along. Perhaps not in all the detail, but the basic understanding was good enough!

The things that made me take stock, to question what I was doing – even to the extent that they made my very foundations tremble a little, was the way that the teachings in question were shown to be misguided and unreliable. A few were the rocks that part of my life and understanding was built upon, and were now shown to be made of, if not sand, then some sort of foundation that was not strong enough to take the weight of the future.

As a species, we have an insatiable need for information, and we like to think that it is correct. Experience tells us that this is not so, and then we become confused and unable to differentiate between the correct and the misleading.

God and Jesus have recognised this plethora of misguided information and our resulting confusion, and see the urgent need to give us an accurate and clear message of how we should be behaving and treating others.

They recognise that people are leaving the established church in droves as the messengers within are not providing fulfilment to our soul and our consciousness. The *"Teachings of God"* need to be brought alive again, and this book is the first major step in that direction. Jesus *is* channelling through the author as the spokesman of God; they cannot be ignored.

There are good things in all of the chapters. Many of them are almost common sense (but that seems to be something that is often lacking as people chase unreal goals in life), of course we should look after the aged better, community care has to be improved for those who are not capable, we have God's love given to us – let's reciprocate. We must be able to enjoy our lives and give happiness to others, in peace, harmony; and get on with our neighbours.

All of these are really basic things that we should do every day without even thinking about it. Sadly, the very fact that there are chapters on these subjects is a reflection that as a race we are not wholly managing even these basics.

However, the real meat of the book comes in those chapters that I haven't mentioned. I'm not going to list those that made me think, or even shook me. Not because there is some sort of secret and I will be in danger of laying my soul open for attack, but because some of the things that made me pay attention, may be things that you are doing already. Similarly there are those chapters that I can be comfortable with that may be a revelation to others.

We are all different and long may it remain so.

The difference between us is not a reason for mistreating others, or the environment in which we live. We can all have the same basic beliefs of honesty and decency and all that that entails, but that will not make us all the same.

The disciples all had a great belief in Jesus, but the way that they showed that belief and went about its implementation was different for each of them.

We can be just as diverse and still make the world a good place to live.

Read the book and apply the lessons in as much as your ability will allow. Your life will be all the richer for it.

Understanding the Need for God in Your Life

Life is given to us as a formula that we have chosen. God created that formula and then created us as individuals, but the job did not end there because He then entered a contract with us to provide everything we need throughout life to fulfil whatever purpose we chose for our lives. At times this means providing nothing but we cannot question His loyalty to us because we chose how it was to be.

We can look on Him as our parent. He is the parent of our worldwide family and so we owe Him our respect and loyalty too, and as in all families we need to work together for the good of the whole and the individuals within it. Where there are problems and difficulties we must work together to overcome them. Where there is success we must celebrate together. There is a special warmth and sincerity felt when we act as one.

But because of the misinterpretations of some of God's staff and the misplaced values put on material wealth in large parts of the world, God has been pushed to one side. He is viewed as the elderly parent who belongs to another age, and would serve the family better if He were put in a residential home. But that is not true.

Even though we may have broken parts of our contract with Him, He has still carried on fulfilling His part. The problem is that He is now struggling against a tide of apathy and a lust for the material advantages in life.

Serving God may sound old fashioned but it is a basic part of living according to the principles you brought to this life. Every time you help someone, you smile at someone, you recycle your paper and your cans, you care for an animal, you laugh, and you enjoy your day..... each time you are serving God. Every time you commit yourself to helping the planet or any of its inhabitants you are serving God.

It is not a complicated formula for us to remember and it works at all levels of society and understanding. Each one of us can do it. Sometimes we do it and fail to recognise it as serving God. However, we have our part to play in the world family and our parent God is there to help us get it right.

So do not let complicated words or the attitude of those trying to push in between you and God get in the way of the most valuable relationship you have on Earth. It does not diminish the love you feel for anyone else in your life, in fact God's love will enrich your life and fulfil you.

Just remember, God is there for you even when you forget to be there for Him.

Understanding the Messages

You will find that in many parts of Jesus' writings he talks of 'us' and 'our needs'. He speaks as though he is living through events with us, and he is. Although he is the Son of God he has lived amongst us as a man, and I feel this brings a closeness that is very precious. He shares our happiness and our anguish and he faces the problems with us. So never feel he is distant. He is right by you. Just as he is my Brother, he is yours too. Talk to him; share your victories and your defeats, your cherished moments and your worries.

He is a great Brother to have. I find he tells me off, he smiles with me, he guides me and he shares my delight when I get a good result. He is a special part of my life and my pathway is so rewarding now thanks to him. I trust him implicitly. Do the same and your life will take on a rich dimension.

Some may feel that the words used by Jesus are out of date for our current lives. The truth as I see it is that we have compromised many of the meanings in our day to day speech. We give different meaning to words, we shorten them. In fact, words are even abbreviated into the letters that start them. For all the attraction of quick communication via the web and mobile texting, we have lost some of the beauty of our language. Yet there must be a need for it at times because there are many recent films that portray an old tongue and they are understood and valued. I wish we could say the same of our English language.

However, I have found that at times there are simply no other words to express the full richness of Jesus' writings. I can offer help with the 'Key Points' and in my 'Clear Accounts' which you will find at the beginning of each writing, but there are many texts where any replacements simply compromise the full meaning. They actually water it down. So please try to persevere with Jesus' words. Some writings you will find simpler than others. I find it often depends on the depth of the subject.

Also I Have compiled a list of a few of his words which I hope you find helpful.

Helping you to understand Jesus' words

Need

I have become aware since I started working with Jesus that there are two distinct stages in everything action we take.

We generate a need to do something.

We then follow that through with the action.

Examples of the use of the word 'need':

'And that of the need now is to teach fulfilment. This means 'It is necessary now to teach fulfilment.'

'For they are of need to learn that which is joy within' means 'They need to learn the feeling of joy within'.

Worth

This too is a word of paramount importance in the writings I am given. It relates to:

The value of something or someone. It may be your spiritual stature. A 'Feeling of Worth' can be said to be 'Feeling Worthwhile' but I feel it is even more than that.

It can also relate where you would use the word 'Quality' as in the sentence, 'It was a quality not many people possessed'.

To say that someone has the money and the worth to make changes, you are saying that they are in a position both financially and spiritually to make changes.

To say that something is of unreal worth means that it is not at all worthwhile.

Career

He often uses this word for the work you do on your pathway, but he does also relate it to the work people do.

Knowing

In certain contexts Jesus uses this as a noun. When he gives me the words in a prayer, 'In thy knowing' it means 'In thy name'. Sometimes it can refer to a being.

Survive

He tends to use this where we use the word 'Live'. It is the basic fact of living, describing both a basic existence and one where there is wisdom and worth.

Before we begin, I feel that you will enjoy and benefit from learning more of Jesus through his own words. It is a writing I channelled on the 25 May 2007.

About Jesus

It is good now to be of service to the educating of Jesus' role in the World when he was born man, to be of service first to live as a carpenter, and then finally to be the Messiah as he lived when he was established to the Worth of God.

For he came not to absolve the sins of the people about him, but to absolve the sins and irresolute characters of those who lived in the World as a whole.

And that character was never resolved to accept a lighter finality than the way he died, but was resolved to bring about change in a needed fashion to be resolute and worthwhile in his need to serve.

For that of the giving of life was preclusion to the life held before the Grace of God. And it was not his celibacy or attitude that defined his merit, but his ability to perform miracles and to bring about changes that could not be performed otherwise.

But there were more needs than this, and the paramount need was to bring to the people an understanding of God that they may forthwith use.

But that of the need was to hold to blessing also those who were his enemies, and he could not go before the people as a Messiah if he did not believe in absolution.

And so it was that he defied the career of many and became the man that you see now portrayed in some legends and fabrications.

But he was of mettle as a man and he gave forthrightness and worth to every aspect of the work. And he gave of substance to the poor, the needy, and the well off were upset by this pious attitude as he held them responsible for their lack of giving towards others. And they were upset, and they became more upset as he became powerful. For they were the focus of his rage and his anger at the state of unrest within the people. Yet they mocked him and they evaluated him by his appearance which was poor but not worthless.

For he was merited by a fine appearance and he had not a moustache but a beard, and he was seen as a magnificent creature among men. For he was forthright and he was able to stand among men and be with them as one. But he was able also to be distant and forthright if needed.

For it was manhood that created a need for a full religious worth to be seen, so that he may show the people that there was a God and He was magnificent in all senses. And that the giving of God's power was to be of worth to giving the people their freedom from malice and hate and all the upset that befell them.

But that was not enough for some and heralded the anger and abuse of some where their need was for a better life, but not one of Godliness and worth. So they were not worthwhile to the cause and left it.

But there were some who were of value to the full and they shall be heralded as the saviours of society, for they fell not when he died, but rose to be of value to spreading the Word and bringing hope where there was none.

For they were the ones who became his disciples and followed him fully faultlessly through his life and beyond. And they were great, and the greatest of them all was Simon Peter, whom I belied to be my brother at hand.

And he was all giving and of value to the task until he died without mercy in the hands of the ones who persecuted him.

For he was the man beyond whom I see none, and I tell you now that he was my friend and my ally in God's Provision. For the worth of God was seen in many ways and he was to perform some of the finest feats of worth in his lifetime.

Let it be that you know now that I was affected not by my need to die until that time when I held unto the final act. And that constituted the need to hang within focus of my mother and all who adored and loved me during life. To see me at the point of death was terrible. For they were so afraid of the upset it would cause within the heavens at my Father's anger, but also because they were the ones with whom I had lived and loved within the time given for my life.

For I was not given to celibacy because I served God only, but I was not given to serve God in the way of having a family. And that would not perpetuate my soul to another but within myself to remain that I may remain the one who gave all and became what he was finally to be at the side of his Father, and about which many felt he would never become.

But he became all and he became equal to God the Father. And he remains now within God's virtue, the one who came and who saw within the lifetime of a man so that he could take that of absolution for all the sins of the world and bring about change for the people in their expectation of God.

For the resuming of God's values must bring to all people a need to serve and fully bring about the changes by nurturing their spirits and redeeming themselves at the Hand of God.

For they are not fully held in the power of God if they do not bring themselves to Him and vouchsafe that they do bring about that change necessary to fulfil all obligations to God and to life.

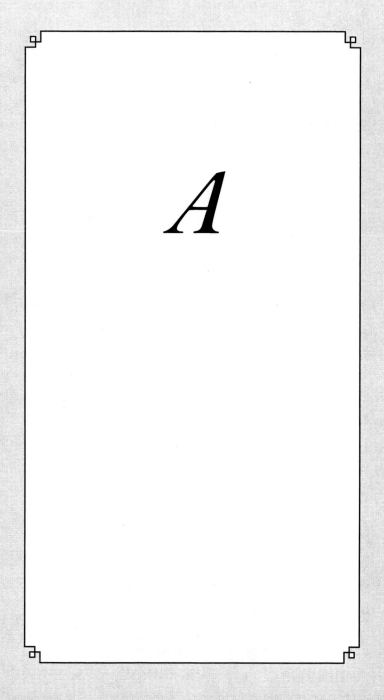

A

Abortion (Channelled 16 May 2007)

Key Points

- A need to mention the horrendous attitude towards abortion.
- There is currently a need to sacrifice life within a person, and a feeling of apathy towards further pregnancies.
- Some will live a liberated life, have sex, but will not have a resulting child, so they sacrifice the life within them.
- It is part of life that we are able to bring life to others and, if the population if to grow, we must fulfil that.
- No part of God's law gives a need to stop a pregnancy.
- Equally no part of God's law stops a foetus from living in a mother's womb until it is born normally.
- It acquires life within the womb and is made within God's mercy. Progress requires change and that given is there to change a life.

- Where there is rape, disease or distress within the limbs of the baby or within the womb, termination may be held.
- On many occasions a woman needs to have a baby but she is afraid it will be unwelcome and unloved.
- Where there is life, there is love for life.
- All loss of life is upsetting and there is a need to generate love within the womb, generate fulfilment and determination for good.

A Clear Account

Jesus says that abortion is unpleasant but cannot be done away with, however it must be thought about carefully. He says there is an horrendous attitude that leads to the sacrificing of a life within a person and leaves them apathetic about future pregnancies, for some will live a liberated life, have sex, and then refuse to have any resulting child.

It is part of life that we are able to bring life to others, and that must be fulfilled if the population is to grow.

There is no reason within God's law for stopping a pregnancy and equally there is no reason for a foetus not to remain in a mother's womb until it is born normally, for it is given life in the womb and is made with the understanding of God. The future must bring change for a person and the life is given so that it changes another life.

You have to understand that where rape has occurred or disease or some distress concerning the baby or within the womb, a termination may happen. But it will value the life as having succumbed to upset and maybe it must then be released.

But often it is meant for a woman to have a baby, but she will not as she believes that the child will be unwelcome and unloved. But where there is life, there must be a love for life and that attitude cannot bring about love but instead people try to manoeuvre God's values so that they fit in with the needs of the mother and father.

You have to understand now that all loss of life is upsetting and it is necessary now to generate love within the womb so that it brings fulfilment and a determined approach to good.

The Writing

Let it be that you write now about that horrendous attitude towards abortion. Let it be that the need to abort has now brought about a need to sacrifice life within a person and bring them apathy about the need for a further succumbing to breeding.

For there are some within life who will go through the needs for sex and be liberal with their lives, but their attitude towards the having of a child will yield not and they bring about change by losing that which is of life within.

For it is a property of life that we are able to bring life to others, and that must be fulfilled if we are to gain in population.

Let it be that you know now that there is no reason within God's Law that shall stop the need for pregnancy. And equally, there is no reason within God's Law where it is said that a foetus may remain not within the mother's womb until it is born normally. For it is without life until it is made within the womb, but then it acquires life and it will be made within God's Mercy. For a way forward must bring about change and that given is to change a life.

Let it be that you understand now that where there is rape and where there has been an understanding of disease or upset within the limbs of the baby or within the womb, that there may be termination held. But it will value the life as succumbing to upset and maybe the need is then to release the upset from within. But there are many cases where the need formulates for a woman to have a baby but she will not as she is given to believe that this child will be unwelcome and unloved. But where there is life there must be a love for life, and that attitude cannot bring about love but a need to change God's values so that they are more like the ones of need to both mother and father.

Let it be that you know now that all loss of life is of upsetting worth and that need now is to generate love within the womb, and to bring about the need to generate fulfilment and a will towards goodness.

Ageism (Channelled 15 June 2007)

Key Points

- Ageism creates upset and is a relic of society.
- In the workplace you are expected to be young if you wish to continue working.
- Some forbid the older generation to be near them or their family, but people must accept that some people want changes in their old age and this is one.
- Some people support the old, but others cause trouble whenever they can.
- There is a need to adjust so that the future can generate good in the name of God.
- Change must begin soon as ageism is bad. It splits families as some members are sent away, whilst others are guilty of banishing relatives.
- There must be a communication between both sides so that everyone who has faith in God learns to change their life.

- The future must not be sad with some living on hate and distress. With God's help we must bring change.

A Clear Account

In this writing, Jesus says that ageism is a derelict part of society and it should be changed to generate something worthwhile instead.

If you are young you can continue to work but power has made some create upset rather than good.

Some are so ageist that they will not allow the old near them or their families. But, whilst they do this, they can never be completely worthwhile until they accept there are many old people who need improvements in their old age and that this is going to mean change. Although many people advocate change some do stir up problems whenever they can.

You have to refocus your mind so that the many reasons for change can be fulfilled and the future can generate good faith in God's name, rather than bad. It should start soon because ageism is a bad thing and there are members of families who banish old relatives, and there are old people who are being sent away by their families.

The Writing

It is good now to talk of ageism for it is a derelict worth in society. And must be brought to a need to generate worth not upset.

Let it be that you are formulated to be young if you wish to continue in work, but that of the giving of power has endowed unto some a need to generate upset and not good.

Let it be that some are so ageist that they will not allow an old person in their sight and they will not allow their family to be upset by them. But they will not be of complete worth until they have accepted that there are many people who are of need to bring about a change that is worthwhile in their old age and that is about to change.

For there are many who advocate a need for old people, yet there are those who bring about upset whenever the need shows.

Let it be that you adjust so that the many reasons can be fulfilled and that the way forth may generate all of good faith and not bad in God's knowing. Let it be soon that it starts for ageism is a bad thing and there are those in families who banish and are banished. Let it be soon that this starts.

Angels (Channelled May 2007)

Key Points

- Angels can enhance someone's life, because their help is outside the normal area.
- The world has never before needed the angels' help so much to clear the contempt that has developed.
- At birth an angel can visit to help influence future decisions.
- Your belief in the angels governs whether you call on them to impact on your life.
- Some people see the benefit but some do not.
- If speedy restoration is needed on a life, the angels may be called to help it.
- Angels influence your choices in life and help if you are misdirected.
- Archangels rearrange the world according to God's code.
- An angel cannot interfere without God's permission, but once that is received they bring immense power.

- Only angels can give life a glow and they shine out in authority.
- Angels can bring love where needed and can restore love if it is needed and right for the situation.
- There are four types of angel including archangels, Cherubim and Seraphim.
- Cherubim and Seraphim are closest to God and bring His Light to the world.
- When failure threatens the world it cannot prevail against the power of the angels.
- Calm is needed and brought sometimes by the angels but they also bring upset when a fear of doing wrong brings change and restores good.
- Archangels are often called on to bring method and wisdom to people.
- It is necessary to bring more of the loving power of the angels to people.
- Your guardian angel stays with you throughout your life, to empower you so that you find laughter, fun and power.
- You have authority over your own life so you must invite angels into it. They will help you cherish power.
- Tell everyone that angels are there for them to use.

A Clear Account

Jesus says that it is good to talk about the work of the angels because it can enhance a person's life if they know that there is help outside the normal area you think of.

For there is a need as never before to bring the angels' help to the world to clear the contempt that has developed in it and restore it to where it is worthwhile to God's gifts.

You must understand that an angel can visit at your birth to bring a change that will influence greatly your decisions later in life, but it is up to you whether you believe in the power of the angels and whether you will call on them when you need help to smooth your pathway or have a different effect. Some can see clearly that angels can help restore a worthwhile situation, but others cannot. You must understand that there is a need to formulate your work before you embark on your life. It may be that a person has an enchanted life restored to them, which earlier they would have considered unthinkable. The process of restoration may require that life is cherished, however it forms and that there must be change as the value grows. If it needs to grow quickly the angels will have to help it and they will bring whatever power is necessary to achieve it, for the formula has to grow accurately so that any later choices are lighter.

Angels influence your choices in life if they know that you are misdirected, and they can instigate changes if necessary. Angels are not all the same; they serve different purposes. Archangels are there to rearrange the world so that it follows God's code.

An angel cannot interfere without God's permission, but once that is in place, they bring an immense power to a situation, so that there is no trauma to God's governing, but instead an exemplifying of His need to govern all things. The angels are the only beings able to give life a glow where necessary and they shine out in authority. They also bring love to a situation where change is needed to win someone's attention. If it is right and it is needed they can restore love in a situation where it is lacking.

There are four types of angel and the archangel is one. There are also Seraphim and Cherubim and they are nearest to God, bringing His Light to the world, for there are areas of worth aimed at bringing failure to the world, but they do not fare well against the angels. Other angels exemplify life according to the will of God. They bring a wealth of value that can immediately bring changes to a world like calming or even an upset. For not only is calm needed but also a fear of doing wrong if that will bring about change and restore good.

Where some need to call on an angel for help they will often be given an archangel to change a situation completely and it may show a person where they can be more worthwhile than they were previously. It is necessary to bring the loving power of the angels into people's lives more, for they will formulate a better life if they are able to grow with the love and value of an angel.

You must understand that the guardian angel you feel beside you at birth is there for you all your life. And that power is not there to interfere with your life, but to empower it so that you discover laughter, fun and power, or whatever you need. In that way the future brings a lifetime's security and is truly worthwhile. The angel will help you to cherish the power you have, but first of all you must invite it into your life. For it is you that has authority over your life, and so you must choose how you are going to make changes and evolve.

Now that you know that the angels are there in your life you can tell everyone that they are there for them to use.

The Writing

It is good to talk about the angels' work because it can enhance a life to know that help exists that is outside normal power, for a need now shows to bring the angels' help to the world like never before, to restore a worth held to obliterating the contempt held to the past and restore a world that is of worth to God's gift.

Let it be that you understand that an angel can call upon you at birth to bring a change to your life that will influence you to a great extent with decisions later in life. But it is up to you if you believe in their power and if you do, whether you call upon them at the times needed to smooth a pathway or impact on your life in a different way, for it is apparent to some and not others that a way exists that shall be worthwhile if it is given the help of the angels to restore worth.

Let it be so that you understand now a need to formulate a career within life fully before that life is given. If it is enchanted, a life may be restored to a person that earlier they held unthinkable to their need. That restoration process may bring a need to cherish life in whatever form and bring a change as that need to be of worth formulates and grows. If it is necessary to grow fast it will be the angels' need to help grow that life and its ability to restore power will be held to their need to bring whatever power is essential to it in growth. For that formula must be accurate and it will not be without a need to grow within in an accurate way so that the growth may be of wisdom of worth held to a lighter and further choice later.

Let it be you know now that the angels influence your choices in life if they know that you are being misdirected, and they can bring adjustment if a need shows for it to be given.

Let it be that you know that all angels are not the same and they serve different purposes. Let it be that the archangels are there for an angelic host that rearrange the world according to a need to be of complete worth to God's code. For an angel cannot interfere if they are not given permission by God to do so, but that need shown they will bring immense power to a situation so that it may traumatise not a Kingdom of God's doing but may exemplify His need to govern the state of all things.

Let it be known that a direct worth held by the angels is to give life a glow where it is needed, to shine forth in an authority of worth. And it cannot be found otherwise than by their own worth held. Let it be you know also that the angels are there to bring a light forth to all proceedings of the heart, for they will bring love to a situation where a need holds to change that situation and bring favour with someone. If it is deemed respectable and a needy worth it can be that love is restored to a situation where love was lacking.

Let it be that there are four types of angel and the archangels are but one. Let it be that the seraphim and cherubim are the ones nearest the throne of God to bring His worth to the light of the world. For a need shows that there are a generation of worths held to bring in failure into the world and they shall not fare well if they are given the power of the angels to combat.

It is well that you also look at the need of the other angels too to exemplify life as is the Will of God. For that exemplification brings a store of worth that can bring forth changes to a world like an instant calming or an upset held to bring change. For it is not only a calm that is needed but also a fear of doing wrong if it will facilitate change and therefore the good is restored if a need is shown.

Where those who are of need, call upon an angel for help they will be given often an archangel who will bring the method and wisdom needed to combat a situation. If it is a desire a person may call upon an archangel to change a situation completely and it can bring a fuller picture of where a person may be of worth than before.

Let it be that you understand fully that a need shows to bring the loving power of the angels more into the lives of everyone, for they will formulate a better life if they are growing with the love and worth held to an angel's power. Let it be so that you know that the guardian angel that you feel beside you at birth is to be there for your complete life and you will find that that power given is in need not to invade your life, but to empower it, so that it is a way to bring laughter, fun, power or whatever circumstance necessary to your life for a way forth that shall establish security and worth for a lifetime.

Let it be that you know too that the angel shall bring you a cherishment of power if you let it, but you must begin by inviting it into your life first, for you are of direct authority to your own life and that must mean that you choose how to bring forth changes and where you need to evolve. Let it be that you understand fully about the angels now in your life and bring forth the news in abundance that they are there for everyone to use.

Archangels (Channelled 19 June 2007)

Key Points

- Archangels are around us day and night, bringing God's values to people.
- They are a valuable asset to the world. They stimulate our progress to bring rapid development when needed.
- Metatron is the archangel specifically responsible for stimulating growth. Hold him in your heart for he is valuable to you.
- Value all archangels. They help you to be worthwhile. They help create good in your life.
- They are an infinite force that helps you to triumph in what you need to do.
- Archangels are messengers. They are a working part of God's force, and give the world a boost when it needs one.
- They also work in parts of the galaxy hidden to man, where there is a need for more light and wisdom.

- Commit to bringing God's Light to all areas of the world. Archangels work there to generate goodness in line with God's kindness and worth.

- Archangels will be around at the end of time, when there is no more evil. They will always be there as God's force against evil so that His force is seen in its full majesty throughout the world.

A Clear Account

Jesus tells us here that the archangels are around us day and night and they bring pleasure to many people by providing them with God's values.

You need to understand that the archangels are a valuable asset to the world. They help us to be rational and they do the same within the world, because the formulae within us all governs our value in the world and also our value to God's work. If we allow it to happen, these values can change our lives. They bring us our ambition, laziness, distress and the good we feel. They stimulate progress and we have to adhere to these values at all times.

Sometimes creating something bad prompts change, equally creating something good can at times bring chaos if it is not appropriate. We do have to bring about change, but if we fail to follow some of the pathways given to us, we cannot create the change because the formula is not right. But the archangels stimulate our progress and can bring rapid development.

Metatron is the archangel specifically responsible for stimulated growth in the world. He is very important to your work. He brings you a future of growth and excellence so hold him in your heart for the value he brings. In fact, value all archangels. They all have excellent properties and if you allow it, they bring you an ability to be worthwhile. They will come when you are stressed and upset and they will help you create good in your lives. For immediately there is a visible need they will be there to bring about change and that is good. Value the good within God's own record as it is responsible for all changes in the world.

You need to commit to God's pathway and you need to be dedicated about it, and they help you to do that willingly, and that is how they serve God's wisdom.

You need to know about the archangels as beings as well as how they play a part in your life, for each is there as an infinite force bringing change to our lives in accordance with our need to succeed or fail, but also so that we may be triumphant and fully effective in what we need to do. You must understand that they are messengers. They are a working part of God's force. Sometimes the world needs a boost and the angels have the best way of doing that. They can overcome evil and are valuable whenever and wherever they are needed. They work in the galaxy as well as here on Earth. There are parts of the galaxy where there is a need to create more light and wisdom. These are areas which are hidden from the human race.

So do not succumb to laziness but instead commit to bringing God's Light to all areas of the world. That is where you will find the archangels. They work where people need converting to good, and where goodness needs generating so that it is in line with the kindness and worth of God. They are there and they will be at the end of time when there is no more evil to be had, only good. This is their formula, the formula for good, and they will always be there as God's force against evil so that His force can be seen fully and majestically throughout the world.

The Writing

This writing deals with the work of the archangels. For they are about us day and night, and they bring to many people a pleasure felt in the wisdom of God's worth held.

Let it be that you understand now that these beings are a valuable asset to the world as they rationalise some areas of worth within us and also the world. For there are formulae held to all of us that dictate our value in the world and to God's work. Let it be that you understand that these values bring about changes in our lives if we allow them, for they are the things that give us ambition, laziness, upset and good felt, for they are the giving of worth to all people in the need to stimulate progress and they must be adhered to at all times.

Let it be that you understand that a generation of upset can bring about change just as a generation of good can bring about chaos where it is not appropriate. Let it be that you know now that there is a need to follow some pathways given and if it is not done we cannot bring about the change needed for the formula has not been successful. But a need to generate worth comes from the archangels whereby they stimulate our progress and can bring rapid development.

Let it be that you know now that there is a need to stimulate growth throughout the world and it is given to us by one archangel in particular and that is Metatron. He is of great importance in your work and he will bring you a way forward of growth and excellence. Let it be that you hold him in your heart for the value he brings. Let it be that you value also the excellent properties of all the archangels and realise that they are there to bring you a great worth felt if you will allow it. For they will come at times of stress and upset and bring to you a need to generate good in your lives. For as soon as the need shows, they are there to bring about change and that is good.

Let it be that you evaluate the goodness of God's own Chronicle that shall be of worth to all changes in the world. Let it be that you know now that there is a need to stand fast in the pathway of God and they give us a need to partake in the willingness to serve so that they may be of value to God's wisdom held.

It is necessary to talk of them as they are and not how they will partake in your life. For each value is needed in the infinite form necessary to bring about change to our lives, that we may succeed or fail but with the attitude of a hero learned and accurate by the full effect of that given.

Let it be that you know now that they are a messenger and a working part of God's force, for that of the need sometimes is to give the world a boost, and that can be given best by the formula held by the angels, for they are a force that overcomes evil and shall present a great value wherever and whenever the need shows. They are present in all our lives and our need to impress on the world that we are a feature to be reckoned with can bring unto them a mission that shall eradicate the bad and formulate the good in us, for they are of value not only to the needs of the world in which we live, but also to those areas of the galaxy where there are hidden worths from man and a need to generate light and wisdom to those who live within.

Let it be that you bring not apathy to your life by showing a need to succumb to the attitude that laziness rules, but attitudinally direct your thoughts to a need to generate the will of God throughout the world so that the Light of God shall shine through. And it is there that you will find the archangels, where there is a need to convert someone to good and where there is a need to bring about good so that it evaluates well with the kindness and worth of God.

For there they are and there they shall be at the end of all time when there is no more evil to be had but only good, for a formula to be of worth unto good is the need of all archangels and they shall be the force of God against evil throughout all time so that the force of God may be seen in full and in the majesty needed throughout the world.

Ask the Angels
(Channelled 3 May 2007)

Key Points

- Never feel you are alone. You never are.
- You cannot manage without angels.
- You sometimes need God's help.
- Angels are around us, angels can bring laughter.
- If you are frightened by the size of a bill, ask the angels for guidance.
- There may be a problem that will delay you on the road. Consult the angels before you leave.
- Angels bring solace and worth to create you a better future.

A Clear Account

Never feel you are alone for you never are. The presence of angels can help your life, and you cannot manage without them. They bring solace and worth which are necessary to your soul.

You cannot be good at everything. It is necessary sometimes to ask for God's help and there we speak of the angels.

They are around us at all times and if you only need to joke and laugh they can bring laughter to your soul.

If a bill frightens you, ask the angels for guidance, on how to pay, or help to source the funds.

Traffic may delay your journey, but by asking for their help as you leave you can avoid this, perhaps by taking a different route.

Ask the angels for their guidance for they are there to help you and to make the future better for you.

The Writing

Never feel you are alone, for you never are. And it is necessary now to tell you how the manifesting of angels can help your life.

For you are able to manage not without angels. They are there with you, and they bring a solace and worth necessary to your soul.

For you cannot be able at everything you do, and it is necessary to ask for help sometimes, and that may be to manifest God's help.

But it is the angels' help of whom we speak, and we are able to manifest them too. For they are there around us at all times, and that need to jest and to be of worth to laughter can bring a call to the angels to bring laughter to your soul.

It may be that you are aghast at a bill's size, and you manifest the help of the angels so that they will bring guidance on the matter.

As you drive, you may be held up by some blockage, but if you ask first, you may feel a need to divert earlier than then and may avoid a backlog of traffic.

Let it be you ask the angels and manifest them so that they are worthwhile to your needs. For they are there to help you and bring you solace and worth so that the way forth is better for you.

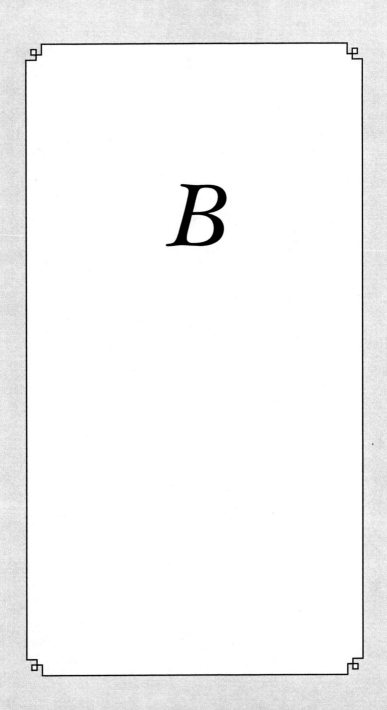

B

Be Dynamic (Channelled 16 May 2007)

Key Points

- Many people may be taught the same things but some feel it is not important to be active.
- The human race is divided between those who believe dynamics are an act of principle and those who think it a needless waste.
- Where a person is educated and eloquent they can be more lively but they must combine that with ease and simplicity.
- Upset and conflict drain a person's energy and self-motivation.
- Aggravation halts progress.
- Panic disables you from the most powerful energy – God's energy.
- Use God's energy if you are able.

A Clear Account

Jesus tells us here that others who are willing to learn may be taught the same as you, but the need to be go ahead and lively is not always thought to be important.

We can look on the dynamics of the human race as an act of principle or a needless waste, yet if we pull our weight as individuals we make life easier on ourselves.

A person may be eloquent and well educated, but combined with the ability to carry power and position you need to create a simple and easy pathway. For if you do you will make the future easier for yourself. However, issues can loom which create problems for you and they can drain your energy and self motivation. For the force of dynamics demands a way clear of aggravation and distress if it is to be successful.

Disruptions halt progress and then speed needs to be built up again.

So remember next time you resort to panic, that you are disabling yourself from the most powerful energy alive – God's energy. Be aware that the energy of God is available to everyone and is freely available to you to use. If you ask, He will provide.

The Writing

That which you are taught is given to others too, if they are willing. But that need to be dynamic is not always thought of as important.

For the dynamics of mankind can be a principled act or a needless waste. It is up to each and every one of us to pull our weight and that can be done and ease our way if we allow it.

For the dynamism of a person is a greater force if they are eloquent and well read, but the need of the mighty may show a need also to generate a pathway that is simple and easy to follow.

If that is the case, the way ahead is easier and not held to conflict, but if the issues in a person's life lead to upset, it will be a draining force on his energy and dynamism. For the force of dynamics demands that a way shall hold where a person may entail not aggravation or upset if they are to achieve a fully dynamic way forward.

If they must suffer aggravation it will apprehend the way forth and bring a need to generate more speed again. It is fullness of character that dictates this.

So let it be that when you next enable yourself a moment of panic or upset that you remember you are disabling yourself from the most powerful energy alive and that is God's, for He will provide and you will use this in full if you are able.

Be Inspired (Channelled 14 May 2007)

Key Points

- It is better to find inspiration in the words said by many than to concentrate only on one. Between them, they may hold the key to your future.
- Many words glorified by man do not generate good.
- Some see themselves as visionaries, but bring upsetting messages, which go on to create even more upset.
- Some do inspire and they must be given the freedom to do so and generate good.
- Listen and work with that which is appropriate and helpful to you.
- Find fulfilment through those who speak the wisdom of God's words.
- Appreciate the value of good words and follow them, instead of the unwise guidance of those who bury God's values.

A Clear Account

Jesus says that any single source of wisdom can inspire you but it is better to accept the words of many, because they can help you and may even hold the key to your future.

Many words glorified by man do not have the right qualities to generate a worthwhile future. Some suppose they are visionaries but see trouble, which then creates even more distress and unfulfilled dreams. Others are good and they must be seen and heard so that a better future is achieved.

Listen fully to that which is given but only work with what is appropriate and worthwhile to you. You will find fulfilment through those who see God's words and not turmoil.

Just realise how valuable good words are and follow them rather than the efforts of some to try and bury God's values.

The Writing

You can become inspired in any one worth, but it is more advantageous if you can accept the good worth shown by many people, because they have the many words necessary to bring you faith in the future. And they may hold the key to your future that you do not know yet.

Let it be soon that you realise that there are many words said that are glorified by man and may not hold good properties to generate worth in mankind. But some are good and they must be heard and read in order to provide a better fabric of worth for the future.

For there are those who suppose they are visionaries and they may not hold the future of worthwhile times and enjoyment but an upset that generates even more upset and unfulfilled dreams.

But there are those that inspire and they must be given free rein to inspire, so that the way forward may generate goodness.

Let it be that you listen fully to that given and only work with that which is of obvious worth to you.

For you will find fulfilment through the words of those who can see the wisdom of God's Words and not upset.

Be Worthy to God
(Channelled 22 May 2007)

Key Points

- It is necessary to hear from the Son of God about the need to be worthy to God

- Jesus has seen many changes since he came to Earth. The most upsetting concerns the hurt to God's pride and the world's needs.

- God must be made worthy again to many people.

- Worship has moved from God and towards money.

- There is a need for some to redress the balance and worship the Father.

- Many are upset they cannot find God within the sanctimony of a church and yet He is there.

- Within the church there are many doubts about who can be trusted to pass on God's word.

- People leave in droves because of dissatisfaction.

- The problem will not be solved until mankind finds someone who will translate the teachings and bring it alive to them.
- Those who should give the Word of God fail to do so.
- The Scriptures are given in a way that upsets people and that is not good.
- They will not be believed until the truth is once more given.
- The Word of God must be true and it must be wise.
- We seek the truth in the Word of God.
- We trust the Might of God to bring the importance and worth to our lives through the message.
- We cannot ignore the needs of those who would be true if they knew the real wisdom of God.

A Clear Account

Jesus' words speak here of the problems of being worthwhile to God and he says that those who need to address the problem need to hear about it from the Son of God. For there have been a lot of changes in the many years since he came to Earth and the most upsetting of all concerns the hurt to God as the superior being, and also the attitude towards the world's needs.

For God must be protected and made valuable again to many. The aversion to worship has been a big disappointment. And yet they cannot see that the reason for not being worthwhile to God can be because of the worship of money, and the human race cannot see how this can bring about such a great change in the world where areas now do not see the need for worship.

It is time for some of them to change their focus and worship the Father more and it will be an ongoing battle until balance is restored in the world.

Many are distressed because they cannot find God within the sanctimony of the church, and yet God is always there.

It should not be that God cannot be provided when there is a need. He is the one in whom everyone trusts and all people are made to feel well again. However there are many doubts as to who is reliable in church when it comes to God's thinking and also who is to be trusted to give His Word.

In the past some have not been satisfied, and they are walking away in droves because they cannot find fulfilment. And it will not be right until mankind finds someone to translate the teachings of the Word of God and bring it alive for them.

Those who should be passing on the Word of God fail to do so and that has to stop, for the fulfilment of the scriptures of the Word of God are given now in a way that upsets people and that is no good. There is no truth in it, and they will not be believed until the people are again given the truth. It will then be believed.

The Word of God must hold truth and wisdom. It must encourage people to reach out and also feel that any commitment is trustworthy and worthwhile.

We seek truth in the giving of God's Word so that we can really believe. We trust in the Might of God to provide a message of significance and importance to our lives. We cannot ignore the needs of those who would be true if they could learn the truth of God's teaching.

And now is the time to teach and bring people a need to progress and learn that which is important to them, for they are given the truth through this work and we will bring to the fore the Message of God so that it is seen to be true.

The Writing

It is good now to address the problems of creed, for it is an attitude that those who need to address it must hear from the Son Of God.

For he who came to the world so many years ago has seen so many changes within the world, and those that are of most upset are those about the realm of God's pride hurt and those of the attitude to the world's needs.

For God must be protected and made worthy again in many eyes, where that of aversion to the needs of worship have given rise to an abundance of upset where those of God's worship are concerned.

And they cannot see how the failure to be of worth to One so great can happen, other than by the worship of man becoming so adulated towards money. And the greed of mankind cannot see how that upset can bring about a change so great in the world that it can no longer sustain a worshipful gaze in some areas.

And is there a need for some to adjust their gaze and become more worshipful to the Father where that attitude prevails? It is certain that this is true, and it must be an ongoing battle until that is restored that is of balance to the world.

For there are many who are upset because they cannot find a God within the sanctimony of a church. And that cannot be, for God is there.

And there cannot be upset in the need to provide God in whom all trust and are made to feel well again.

But within a church there are many doubts who is to be of stable approach unto God's thinking, and who is to be trusted in the giving of His Word. For that giving past has not satisfied some and they are walking away in droves, for the fulfilment of mankind's needs has not been met. And it will not be met until mankind finds a person who will translate that of the teachings of the Word of God and bring it alive to them.

For they are not giving, who should give of the Word of God, and that cannot be. For the fulfilment of the scriptures of the Word of God are given now in measures of upset, and that is not good. For there is no truth in the measures, and that given shall be believed not until the truth is given once more to the people and it is believed.

For that of the Word of God must hold truth and it must hold wisdom. And it must give ambition to reach forth and feel that commitment given is trustworthy and worthwhile.

For it is in the giving of the Word of God that we seek truth; that we may truly believe that given to us. And it is in the Might of God we trust for the message to bear importance and worth to our lives. For we cannot continue the forbearance of some who would be true if they could learn the truth of God's learning.

And that need now is to teach and bring to the people a need to move forward and learn that which is important to them.

For they are given the truth through this work, and we will bring forth the message of God, so that it is seen in truth and heard in love and given in worship.

For it will bring you a need to serve God's Pathway, and it will give you a worshipful way towards that of goodness and worth in your life, so that you may benefit and fulfil your life in the goodness of God's Mercy.

Let that of your need now bring about changes to your life so that your attitude is worshipful and loving to the future; so that you benefit in the Worth of God and He is brought to you in truth and worth so that the way forward is given in true measure to that which you need.

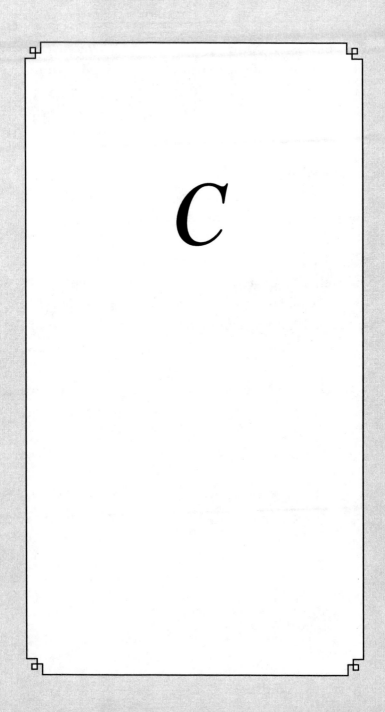

C

Change Your Life
(Channelled 6 June 2007)

Key Points

- Some people live through hell in the pursuit of money.
- It takes time and adjustment to improve your life. The change needs to be appropriate.
- Change can be instant, but you need to be able to look back and see the difference.
- God does not intend to upset you, but the process might. It may involve failure.
- You may instigate immediate change and clear your concerns.
- Good does not always come without pain.
- The process can bring a worthwhile and good change to your life.
- Formulate your life to bring good and not failure.

A Clear Account

There is a living hell that some people put themselves through for money. Hopefully, you are not one, but if you are it will take time and adjustment to improve your life, for the solution never seems good if the change is not appropriate, and you have a dormant period.

It is easy to change your life and serve God's values instantly; however the need at this moment is to change your life so that when you look back you can see the difference. So that means a shake up and that comes with a new and worthwhile formula.

For God does not give you things to upset you, but because you have to formulate a new process, it may upset you. For it is not a happy choice if it involves failure, and if you ultimately wish to serve God that may be the only choice.

You may be someone who manages to bring about an immediate change and that clears whatever has been concerning you. Then everything will be good again. But that is not always possible. Good does not always arrive without pain.

You may have to lose the pride that money brings you. If you do, you need to go in the direction that makes the distress worthwhile. If you do you will discover that the process will bring a worthwhile and good change in your life.

Hopefully you will formulate your life so that it brings good and not failure.

The Writing

It is necessary to talk about the living hell that some people put themselves through for the need of money.

Let it be that you are not one of these, but if you are it will take some time and some conditioning to bring about change, for it never looks good to you if you mis-appropriate change to bring about a dormant time in your life.

For you are able to change your life and bring about a source of God's values in an instant. But that need not to change will bring about a need to evaluate your life so that you can see the difference.

So there is a need for a shake up and that will come about with a need to formulate a substitute of worth to you.

For that which is given to you by God cannot be of upset, but that need now to formulate the procedure may bring about upset. For it cannot be a happy choice if it is to bring about failure, and that can only be done if the one of need to change can bring about a need to serve God ultimately.

Let it be that you are one who will change in an instant that which has been bothering you; so that it may be of upset no more. Then that which is of goodness can abound.

However, it is not always possible to bring about good without that of pain, and it must be that if you are about to lose that dignity of worth within your life that is led by money alone, that you must bring about change that is needed to give out solitude of life that can be of worth to upset. So let that of worth hold unto you and bring you abundant and worthwhile change.

Let it be that you formulate your life now so that you are about to countenance good and not failure in your life.

Changing Attitude
(Channelled 25 May 2007)

Key Points

- People must change their attitude if the world is to retain some sanity and not be swallowed up by lust and hate.
- Lust and hate governs some areas. Some resist changing to a better life as it is easier to cling to the past, but this is no good.
- Arriving in the spirit realms we see the summary of all our sins and not an edited version.
- Our attitude in life moulds our life in spirit.
- To move on to the greatest heights we must wait until our ability reaches new heights.
- We can only build on a foundation that we control.
- We acquire more knowledge in our spirit life than we can on Earth.
- We come to life with the attitude that we can achieve whatever is worthwhile. We then leave the world with a need to build on our knowledge.

- Having to adjust can cause upheaval, but it is essential otherwise the knowledge you can access is restricted.
- Knowledge is paramount.
- God's values must be upheld. They are the framework for yours.
- Upholding the right laws will bring a change in attitude.
- Adjust soon so that you bring great promise and learning to your life.

A Clear Account

Jesus tells us that people must change their attitude if the world is to retain some sanity and not be enveloped in hate and lust. Already it has taken over in some areas, and some turn down the opportunity of a better life because it is easier to cling to the past, but this is no good.

When we pass to the spirit realms, we see the summary of all our sins and not just a list of the good things with a few bad ones thrown in. Our attitude when we pass relates to our life and that moulds our future life in spirit as we move into the realms of learning in our spirit home.

You must understand that we are not allowed to ascend to the greatest heights until our ability reaches new heights. We can only build on that over which we have control, and our career in spirit depends on the attitude we have about the area on which we previously focussed.

Building on that educates us more than we can ever achieve on Earth, so we must have the right outlook so that God's purpose can be seen in the reliable and loving approach we hold. As we achieve, we become more capable and we endure things more easily.

We all come to life with the attitude that we can achieve whatever is worthwhile to us, and when we leave the world we carry on the need to build on our knowledge. Life on Earth can supply some of it and once we reach the spirit realms we are given all we need to bring opportunity and worth to our lives, so that we continue needing to develop.

You will already be aware that having to adjust can cause upheaval in your life, however it is essential because if you are unable to do so you will only be able to access some of the information and that limits the amount you learn and the improvement you gain from it. For if we are to see God's pathway we have to learn enough in the first place so knowledge becomes a paramount need.

God's values must be upheld and you must learn this. They must also provide the framework for the values you hold. If you fail to learn principles such as these, you will find that there is a stern requirement for you to do so and uphold them. Ultimately, living by the right laws will bring about a change in attitude among people. So adjust your life soon and when you learn God's values you will find that you bring to your life a future of great promise and learning.

The Writing

Those who live are to change their attitude if they are to bring a sanity to the world and not envelope it in hate and lust. For that is what has taken over in some quarters, so there are many here who will not hold to a better life if they are given the option, but will instead decide to follow the line of least aggravation to them and cling to the past. But this will not do, for it is the summary of all sins that we see when we pass and not that of a narrative that gives us the good parts and the knowing of some bad but not all. For that which is relevant to us in life is our attitude in passing, and that will mould our future life in spirit as we tread forth the realms of learning within the spirit home.

Let it be that you know now that we may not ascend to the greatest heights until we have seen our own ability launch forward to new heights; and that we can only build that which we have governance over. For the need to build a career within spirit is to be attitudinal towards that dimension where we have worked before, and the need to build on that brings us learning that we can never achieve on Earth. Therefore it is essential that we have the right character approach to build on the need to be stalwart and loving so that God's purpose can be seen. And that achieved can go towards our worth for the way forth, so that we are more able and enduring.

Let it be that you know now that we come with the like mind that we can achieve whatever is of purpose to us, and when we leave the Earth we bring with us a need to learn more. For that given on Earth can only bring partial knowledge and that equipment that we need to learn more in the direction is given throughout our life in spirit, so that we can bring opportunity and worth to our lives and a need to develop further.

Let it be that you have learned before that a need to adjust can cause aggravation but that need is paramount, for without it the access to information is limited, and that given can only partially effect an improvement in learning. For the giving of knowledge is paramount if we are to learn enough that God's pathway can be seen.

Let it be soon that you learn that God's values have to be held to and they must provide the framework for all values held. Let it be soon that you learn also that a dereliction of duty towards the learning of such principles will bring about a stern requirement that knowledge be given and upheld.

Let it be soon that you learn that God's values are to be upheld and that that can bring about an upholding of the correct laws so that an attitude change can be seen among people. And let it be soon that you adjust your life so that you learn God's values and bring to your life a way forward of great promise and learning.

Climate Change (Channelled May 2007)

Key Points

- Many get upset about the need to be green because it entails work.
- They feel it does not affect them.
- Now it is necessary to care about the environment
- Many are only concerned about their own needs and not the world's.
- Some are dedicated to consumerism which destroys the forests and upsets the very ground on which we stand.
- Loving the environment will require colossal changes but this will anger the very communities it is helping.
- The world's climate will change but the ones who use cars and live comfortably want their needs satisfied first.
- Money must be spent.
- The future of the world is in peril and must be saved.

- The animals of the world must be rescued and their habitat returned to them.
- Crops are so full of chemicals they affect the environment through emissions.
- There is a need to return to organic farming.
- People must see that they cannot ruin the world and live happily ever after.
- Some destroy the good created by those who lived before. That cannot be.
- Pay attention to the needs of the forests and the clean air.
- Love the world.

A Clear Account

To many the issue of being green is upsetting. They do not want the added work and they feel that they are already responsible citizens so it cannot apply to them anyway. But there is a need to act now to save the environment and sustain growth.

Many only think about themselves and not how things affect the world. They are wrapped up in consumerism which destroys forests and upsets the very ground on which we stand.

Loving the environment involves colossal change and this will anger the very people it serves. The world's climate is to change and those who want improvement will not see it because the needs of those who use cars and live comfortably have to be satisfied first.

You must understand that large amounts of money must be spent and the anger dispensed with, for the future of the world is in peril and it must be saved.

It must be everyone's aim to rescue the animals of the world and return them to their rightful habitat. Every person must help in the face of climate change so that it does not take over the world to the detriment of all species.

There must be a need to change to the organic farming of our ancestors and not grow crops that are full of chemicals that affect the environment through emissions.

It is necessary to offer a stagnant world the opportunity to live again so that the world is not divided or upset by change. In that way God's love can bring about the changes necessary to the environment so that it is once again seen as essential to be green.

You must learn soon that there is no way back if you burn all the palm forests in your tank and yet only restore a small part of the world, because we speak of the whole planet, and people's logic must tell them that they cannot ruin the world and live happily ever after. They will not enjoy an abundance of good crops and healthy trees and foliage, for some try and destroy the good done by people who lived in earlier times and that cannot be if the good is to continue.

Look after your world. Pay more attention to the needs of the forests and the clean air and format a way that brings love back to the world.

Do this soon and give back what is needed.

The Writing

The issue of being green is to many an issue of upset. They are upset about the need to think about something that can only entail work to them. And they think also that it cannot affect them too much as they are laudable characters and held not to offend others.

But that need now is to change the environment so that it shows that we care, and to be of worth also to sustaining that which is growth and not upset.

For there are many in the world who would be upset by being of worth only to their needs and not allowing for that affecting the world, for they are wrapped up in a consumer bound affair that shall bring the destruction of forests and upset the ground on which we stand.

For the formatting of these things is not vainly called loving the environment, but is a need to bring about changes so colossal that it will anger the very community for which it serves, for it is about to change the world's climate and that anger cannot bring a challenge to the ones who need to change for good, but for a change that satisfies the ones who must use cars and live comfortably, for they are to be satisfied first.

Let it be that you understand that money must be spent and that anger must be dispensed with, for the future of the world is in peril and it must be saved.

For a goal ahead must be to rescue the animals of the world and give them their homeland back. And to bring to all people a need to serve climate change, and bring it not a need to take over the world, but to give everyone the need to change through organic farming and not making crops so full of chemicals that they affect the environment through emissions.

And to bring to a stagnant world a need to live again in the truest capacity so that the world is not segregated or upset by change, but so that the giving of God's love can bring about changes necessary to the environment so that once again a need shows to be of green worth to environmental needs.

Let it be soon that you learn that there is no way back if you burn all the forests of palm in your tank and you give only to restore a small part of the world, for it is to all the world that we speak, that we may bring about the accustoming of people's logic so that they see that they cannot ruin the world and live happily ever after, for they will not find the abundance of good crops and stalwart worth of the trees and foliage if they abandon the need to sustain them.

For that given to some is to destroy the good of all those who passed earlier, and that cannot be if the goodness is to prevail.

Let it be that you attend to your world and you pay more attention to the needs of the forests and the clean air, and are given to remedying the way intended for a statutory return to love in the world.

Let it be soon that you do this and give back that which is needed.

Co-existing with other Planets
(Channelled 27 May 2007)

Key Points

- Some are horrified that there may be an alien force around us.
- Beings exist but not in the world at this time.
- Others came in the past to help us progress.
- Some believe all substances have the same origin. This is not true.
- Many planets live around us; we are not alone in the Universe.
- Some planets are alive but do not need water.
- We should not meddle where there is any concern and in one or two planets there is a working problem, man's interference may prompt failure.
- God's Law exists in all living planets.
- Those within their planets are peaceable.
- We must be peaceable. We must allow them their distance.

A Clear Account

Jesus says here that the thought that there may be aliens around us prompts horror in some people. Everyone needs to know that there are beings on another planet and beyond, some just find it all nonsense.

There is only the human race within the world at this time. There have been others who came and brought the need for us to progress and follow God's Will in the way we understand it today.

Some believe that all related substances come from the same part of the same planet, but this is not true. Radiation can bring death in one form but alienation brings life to all those brought together in a need to co-exist.

Some dispute there is life beyond Earth, but many planets live around us. We are not alone in the Universe. Some think if there is not water, there is no life. This is wrong for some planets are fully alive but have lost the need for water. The ground manages without it.

Since ancient times the human race has felt that Earth was the only planet with the potential for life, but there is a lot out there and it will continue as long as we leave it alone as much as possible.

We should not meddle where there is any concern and in one or two planets there is a working problem that could bring about failure if man insists on interfering.

You must understand that God's Law exists in all planets where there is life, and not just on Earth.

Where there is love and worth, it follows that there is understanding.

But war will not happen if there are to be armies of men waiting for aliens to appear. There are only those within their own planet, and they are peaceable and not war like.

We too must be peaceable towards our alien friends, who can bring love or war depending on how we act. We should allow them their distance and not bring the shame to the world never again knowing peace.

The Writing

It is necessary now to talk on a subject that brings horror and instability to some where there is a force held to believe that there is an alien force around us, for the need now is to bring a knowledge to all people that there are those who inhabit another planet and beyond. But there are those also who find the need for extra terrestrial upset a nonsense.

But that is true. There is no force other than our own within the world at this time. But there have been those who have travelled and they have brought to us a need to move forward in life and endure God's will in another form, for there are those who would believe that all inter-related substance must come from the same source of the same planet. But that is not true.

For it is a radiation that brings a concept in dying in one form, but alienation that brings a life to all forces in which we live.

For there are those who will dispute that there is life beyond Earth, but there are many planets that live around us and we are therefore not alone in the Universe.

But there are some who think there cannot be life if there is no water, but there is not truth in this, for there are some planets that fulfil the need completely by abandoning the need for water and relying on that in the ground to endure without.

For it is an optimism held by man since ancient times that he has only to know of the Earth's potential to hold life and not beyond.

But there is much out there and it will continue to exist as long as we disturb it as little as possible, for there is a need not to meddle where there is upset, and in one or two planets there is a functioning upset that can create failure within a time set by man if he cannot stop himself from intervening.

Let it be so that you realise that God's Law exists not only on Earth but in all planets where there is life. And there shall be an understanding of life shared where there is a need for love and worth given.

But that need for war will not infiltrate if there are to be armies of men waiting at the door for those to appear that are of alien form. For there are no others than the ones of need to planetary form and that given is not to war, but to peace.

Let it be that you are peaceable towards your alien friends who may bring love to your planet if they are willing, or that of war if you cannot restrain your need for violence.

Let it be that you allow them their distance and bring not shame upon a character of the world so that it never again knows the peace that is wanted within.

Community Care
(Channelled 23 June 2007)

Key Points

- The long term ill need help when they cannot help themselves.
- Government allows only for short term ill.
- Permanent care is necessary for some war injured, some enduring disease and some of those who suffer mental illness.
- The government must improve the lives of those with these problems, instead of leaving them in miserable conditions.
- Some people feel that those needing help are too difficult to care for.
- You must refocus on providing goodness and God's love for everyone.

A Clear Account

Jesus shows here that he is concerned at the level of care available for some long-term sick. He says that there is a need to provide for the unwell when they are unable to help themselves. The government only allows for those with short term and not serious illness.

Some need permanent care because of injury through war, an inherited disease or some mental illness, which is not serious enough to isolate them, but they need to live a normal life.

There are some who are not really a risk to themselves but they need to be generally looked after, because they cannot manage it for themselves, and those who need to care for them fail to do so.

The government need to make things worthwhile for the people so they experience strength through goodness, because the future cannot be miserable for them, just because they are less able to move around or have a mental illness.

Yet some say they are too difficult to care for and that plans cannot include them.

Understand that you must refocus on a way where there all these people are well cared for according to their needs, and God's love is there for every person.

The Writing

It is necessary now to talk about the need to provide for the unwell when they are unable to provide for themselves.

For that provision made by government is for only those who have a passing illness and not a capital disorder. And there are those who will need care for always because of war or the penalty of an inherited disease, or even those with a mild attack of insanity where it is not enough to provide a secluded area of calm, but they are to participate in ordinary life.

Let it be that you know now that these are people who are at little risk to themselves, save the need to be generally looked after, for they are unable to care fully for themselves, but are not looked after by the ones who need to.

And that of the need now is to bring to the government a need to generate fully that intent to give worth to the citizens and bring about changes to goodness and valour held.

For the way forth cannot be of dismal approach if a person is less able to move around or is of upset to the mind. Yet there are many who say that the way forth cannot include these for they are too difficult to care for.

Let it be you understand now a need to adjust your thoughts to a way where that of goodness is seen and the love of God is held to each person.

Corruption (Channelled 19 June 2007)

Key Points

- There is a need to stop corruption.
- Corruption is prevalent in some areas of the world. That cannot continue if God's worth is to be seen.
- Many people would change if the future offered something better.
- Everyone has the ability to cause trouble and distress, but they will not get involved in it if there is a good alternative.
- Those who need to learn goodness are those unable to follow the way of God.
- Some will not change, but others will if they think a future of goodness is worthwhile.
- You can unify the world through change but not if you are cynical about it.
- There are ways in which those committed to corruption can change. You can change their minds if you explain the huge value of God's presence.

- You can bring changes by telling someone that you know of their corruption.
- Pray together.
- You can act as a catalyst. You can bring the value of God into people's lives.

A Clear Account

Jesus says here that it is necessary to stop corruption, for there is a lot of it and in some areas in particular it is prevalent, but it cannot continue if God's worth is to be seen. There are many who would follow a good path if they were convinced it offered a better future. There is a need to bring good to the world. Everyone has the ability to cause trouble, but if there is a good alternative they will avoid it. Those who need to learn goodness are the ones least able to follow God's way, so it falls on the onlooker to help change that. Some will not change but then others feel it is worthwhile.

So refocus your mind and instead of being cynical, take on the challenge of reforming and unifying the world. There are ways that people can commit to good and it is a matter of changing the values of those involved in corruption so that they can again reach God. You have the ability to change things. Tell people if you know that they are being corrupt. Tell them the value of having God in their lives and pray with them. If you are successful you will change someone to include God in their life. They can then realise first hand that God's love brings the good that nothing else can, so bring God's values to mankind.

The Writing

That of the need now is to talk of the need to prohibit corruption, for there is much corruption in the world and it will not bring goodness to the world.

Let it be that you know now that there is a prevalent force of corruption in some areas of the world and that cannot continue if the worth of God is to be seen. For there are many who would hold to goodness if they were given the need, and the need now is to bring unto them a better more fortuitous future than that of the past.

Let it be you know now a need to bring about goodness in the world and there is a measure of upset in everyone if it is allowed, but a need not to relish upset if the worth is given to be of goodness. Let it be that the ones of need to learn goodness are those who are least able to bring themselves to the way of God, and that must bring a need to fortify all those who see the worth given and are of a need to change that. For there are some who will not change, but there are those where a future of goodness spent is of worth to them and they shall be converted.

So let it be that you adjust your view to that not of the cynic, but of the reformer, whereby you take it unto yourself to bring about change and unify the world. For there are ways set to man that can commit to a good future, and that needed is to change the values of those committed to corruption so that they are again able to communicate with God and bring about change in their lives.

Let it be that you are able to bring about change too, for where you see that which is of upset let it be that you bring about a need for change by calling upon the ones of need to tell them of the event. Where you see corruption, let it be that you allow it not to continue but bring about change in the minds of those corrupters present. Let it be that you alter their mindset by evaluating the presence of God as the greatest value given to man and allow that of the need to place authority on this by sealing that done with a need to pray together.

Let it be that you try this and if it is successful you will be able to bring about change in one who has contemplated not the worth of God but needs to realise that there are many areas of mankind's needs that cannot be formulated without the love of God in its stem. Let it be that you try this and bring the value of God to the wisdom of mankind held.

Create a Happier Life
(Channelled 6 June 2007)

Key Points

- People need to be happier and improve their lives in general.
- Lives are formulated for failure or success so some cannot be happy, but now it is necessary to convert some of the failures to achieve a better life.
- Many borrow from the bank and the result is distressing.
- People become so demoralised it affects their personalities. It is an ongoing process.
- Happy people not only feel worthwhile but they create goodness around them.
- If you are not happy, then take steps to achieve happiness. You can do this by serving God and being worthwhile to others.
- If you help others and serve God He will format a way to make you happy.

- You have many opportunities to be happy and what is given to you cannot be taken away unless God says so.
- Being happy makes you want to create good in your life.
- Do not dismiss the good things in your life and create distress.
- Create yourself a life rich in goodness and worth.

A Clear Account

Jesus states here that people need to be happier and improve their lives generally. He says that lives are formulated to bring failure or success, so it is true that some cannot be happy, but it is necessary now to convert some of those failures so they achieve a better life, and see God's Purpose is for fulfilment rather than upset.

Many would not borrow from others, but they do from the bank and they find the result distressing, because they then sacrifice so much that gave them pleasure in the first place. They cannot then find an alternative route.

The thing is, that forces are then present that demoralise people to such an extent it can affect their personalities, because the distress continues and this can prompt other changes that do not make people happy even though they follow God's values. Later the changes will bring happiness, and a need to serve God will bring a positive change in character.

For happy people are worthwhile in their formula for life, but they also bring goodness around them, so they can be content and happy with what they have.

It is hoped that you are made to be happy, but if you are not, bring changes to your life that show success and make you feel worthwhile, for they are what you need. And you can achieve this by serving God and being worthwhile to others.

Do this and have faith that it will be favourable to God, for He will work out a pathway that brings you happiness. He will not allow you to be miserable if He can prevent it.

You must realise that you have many opportunities to be happy and that will not be taken away unless God allows it. Because it is there to endow your life with great happiness and if you have that you will want to create goodness in your life.

Once you understand this, bring about whatever changes are needed so that you no longer dismiss the worthwhile and good things in your life and create distress for yourself.

Learn this, and then bring about your own changes so that your life is rich in goodness and worth.

The Writing

It is true that many are unable to be happy within their lives, and that cannot be. For there are formulae within people's lives that can bring about failure or success, and that need now is to convert the failures amongst us, and bring about a better life so that they are able to see that God's purpose is for fulfilment and not upset.

For there are many who will not live at the expense of others, yet they are indebted to banks and upset at the formula given, for they have given away most of that which has given them pleasure, and they cannot formulate another pathway that has an upsurge of worth in it.

But there are forces that abound that can take a person to a demoralised state and that can bring about an upset of character. For the need to maintain upset can bring about all changes that cannot bring happiness and yet that shall be of worth to a need to serve God's values, for they will bring about happiness, and a need to serve God shall bring about a change in character for the better. For it is said that a happy person cannot be unreal in their formula for life, but they can bring about a need to change that which is of goodness bound, and bring it about them so that they can be content and happy with their lot.

Let it be that you are formulated so that you are happy, but if not, let it be that you shall bring about changes to your life that indicate success and worth. For they are the features that you need to endow yourself with. And you can formulate this by giving your service to God and being of value to others.

Let it be soon that you do this and abound in faith that that given shall be of favour to God, for He will formulate a pathway that brings about happiness, and

He shall not allow you to be miserable within, if He can bring about those things that prevent it.

Let it be soon that you realise that you have many chances at being happy, and that given can never be taken without God's permission. For that given to you is to endow your life with a happiness beyond reason, and it will bring you a need to generate goodness within your life.

Let it be soon that you realise this and bring about changes so that you no longer dismiss the actions of goodness and worth and bring about upset in life. Let it be soon you learn this and bring about change of your own, so that you may endow your life with properties of goodness and worth.

Create Equality
(Channelled 24 May 2007)

Key Points

- Everyone should communicate love to each other.
- Those who discriminate rather than love are not blessed.
- Everyone in the world is equal.
- God's purpose is to unite everyone in the need to live together and bring knowledge for the benefit of all.
- Wealth should be used to bring changes so that everyone is equal.
- Need creates change.
- Everyone should know that they live the worthwhile life that others enjoy.
- God's values must endure.
- It is necessary to change the outlook of those who believe God does not exist.

- Change your life now and tell everyone that God's purpose has to be lived, and lived in full.

A Clear Account

Jesus emphasises here that everyone needs to express their love for each other. For those who discriminate because of race, colour, belief or even imagined difference, are not blessed because they do not love.

The only differences are in our minds, and we must treat everyone equally. For no matter where they are born in the world they are equal, and just because they are less able to understand some of our wisdom and our power, they cannot be dismissed.

God's purpose is for everyone to unite and live alongside each other, bringing together their knowledge so that everyone benefits.

You must understand that it is necessary for the human race to live worthwhile lives, and not discriminate with the result that some are poor and others wealthy. It is necessary to use that wealth so that all people are equal. In that way God's commitment can be seen as the world benefits.

Need creates change and currently the need is to make changes worldwide, so that each person benefits from knowing they live the same worthwhile life others live, and do not have to endure the stress they face on a daily basis.

God's values must endure and change the outlook of those who believe He does not exist with the result that they will not commit to a need to further their learning.

You should adjust your life and let everyone know that God's purpose is to be lived, and will be lived in the future.

The Writing

It is necessary now to bring to everyone's attention the need to communicate their love to each other.

For they are not blessed who do not love and discriminate between one being and another because of race or colour or belief or even imagined difference, for they are equal who are born in every area of the world. And they cannot be overlooked because they are less able or less understanding of our power and wisdom.

For God's Purpose is to unite everyone in a need to live together and bring together their knowledge and wisdom so that all who hear it may benefit.

Let it be that now you know that the need is to bring worth to all who inhabit the Earth, and not to discriminate wherefore some are poor and others wealthy. But to use that wealth to bring about changes so that all people shall be equal, and the commitment of God may be seen in all attitudes so that the world benefits.

For it is need that creates change, and that need now is to bring forth the changes necessary on a worldwide scale so that each and every person shall benefit from a knowledge held; that he or she may continue knowing that they are given the life of worth that others enjoy, and not just the simplest and upsetting situation that they endure daily.

Let it be that you know soon that God's values must endure and forthwith bring a pragmatic scheme to change the outlook of all who think that God does not exist, and shall not hold to changing them in their need to further their learning.

Let it be soon that you adjust your life and bring to everyone a knowing that God's purpose is to be lived, and will be lived in full in the coming time.

Create Love (Channelled 4 June 2007)

Key Points

- It is necessary to save what is good in the world and develop on it.
- The world must change its thinking and spread more love. A lot has been lost.
- You are a child of God so you must develop the love in your heart.
- To be more worthwhile in life you must bring love to your soul.
- God's goodness is there to develop you, not leave you unchanged.
- Changes must be made that help the world.

A Clear Account

Jesus says here that it is necessary to take what is good in the world and build on it so that more good develops.

The world's thinking must change so that it spreads more love and appreciates the love that is given because a lot of its energy and love has been lost.

You are a child of God so you must develop the love in your heart and to achieve a more worthwhile life you must bring love to your soul. God's goodness is given to you and it must be used to develop you, so that you do not remain unchanged.

Many areas must be dealt with and changes must be made that are positive to the world. You must start this soon.

The Writing

It is now time to talk of the need to bring salvation to the world. For it is to be of worth to a need to salvage that which is good within the world and build on the work done so that it may bring forth good.

For that of the need now is to change the world's thinking so that it may communicate more love and appreciate that which is given to it also. For the benefit of love is to bring about change and worth, and it must be given so that it can generate worth in a world that has lost much of its vigour and love.

Let it be soon that you generate love within your heart for you are a child of God and that need now is to bring love to your soul so that you may generate that of worth within life, for the goodness of God is given and it must generate a worth that brings about change and not stagnant approach to those things that must be altered.

For there are many areas now to attend to and they must be seen in the need to give that of fullness of character and bring about changes necessary to the world.

Let it be soon you start this.

Create Wealth
(Channelled 12 May 2007)

Key Points

- To achieve a better quality life you may put personal needs and those of your family first.
- Is earning more income for visible assets better than bringing a new value to your life?
- Forget the need to earn more and you will feel better.
- Talking about a new car, better house etc., is not fulfilling and does not help others.
- If you are rich and earn income easily, earn for others too.
- Relax in the knowledge that all gifted people can create wealth and it will be an even better world when they do.
- Start soon.

A Clear Account

Jesus says that you may feel obliged to help yourself and your family to a better quality of life, but how do you determine quality? Is it by earning more income so that all the benefits are visible for all to see, or is it by bringing a new value to your life?

For as soon as you modify the need to generate more income purely for yourself you will feel better. There is a pressure from society for a new phone, a new car, a better house etc. but none of these will satisfy the soul nor will they benefit others.

Yet as you benefit, so you can help others too.

Let us say you are rich and easily generate money. Is it not better to do this so that others may also benefit? For thinking only of yourself means that you generate enough for your needs and selfishness will make you keep the excess.

Let it be that you generate enough so that others can benefit too, so that you can relax emotionally and enjoy the release. All gifted people can generate wealth to share and once everyone does, it will be a better world.

Let it be soon that you do.

The Writing

Is your life as fulfilling as you need?

You may feel obligated to help yourself and your family to attain a better quality of life, but how do you determine quality? Is it to be of service to a need to generate money so that all the benefits that come from it can be seen? Or is it to bring a new worth to your life?

For you will generate a new worth as soon as you forget the past need to generate money and hold to feeling better, for the need is there to generate a way forward that gives you a need to talk about a new phone, a new car, a better house etc., but it will not fulfil your brain to do this, neither will it generate an income for the benefit of others.

Yet as you see benefits for yourself you can serve others too.

Let it be that you are rich and able to generate income easily. Is it not better to bring a better life for other people too, for that given to separate thinking means that you generate only as much as is necessary for the task and no more.

Let it be that you generate enough that other lives can benefit too so that you can relax emotionally and enjoy the release that all gifted people can create wealth and it will be an even better world when all do.

Let it be soon that you do.

Criticism (Channelled 16 May 2007)

Key Points

- Criticism can be constructive. It can also be empty.
- There is a temptation to be overcritical and just get upset.
- That given by God cannot be criticised.
- If you cannot recognise good you will not find the future welcoming.
- By giving love we create a nicer future and that brings calm.
- Being fraught only creates upset and anguish. Avoid it.
- Look for good and you will find benefit.
- Do not waste time on upset and anger. Instead generate good and formulate a better future.

A Clear Account

Jesus says that criticism can be constructive but it can also be empty with the consequence that you can over criticise and totally lose your calm. You should stop yourself before it is too late because, firstly, you cannot criticise what God gives you, and secondly, if you intend to live life in a willing way it is not appropriate, so that only leaves you with the option of getting on with things.

If you cannot see good how can you create a welcoming future, and if you are to be worthwhile that cannot be. A troubled life brings only upset and a life of criticism can only leave you with a need to criticise.

When we give our love to each day we create a nicer and worthwhile future and that brings calm. We need to avoid creating anguish, it comes when we are fraught. There is a better way, and if you favour good you will benefit, so do not waste time allowing anger and upset to rule your life. Generate good and worth and you can then formulate a better future.

The Writing

Criticism can be constructive. It can also be empty. And that leads to the temptation of criticising more and not stopping before you are fully upset and unable to calm. Let it be that you apprehend yourself before it is too much.

For that given by God cannot be criticised and that in the mind frame for a life of willing help cannot be criticised, so that leaves only a need to generate that ability to serve and not to criticise.

For the way forth cannot bring a general welcoming tone if the forces of good are not seen, and that cannot be if you are to be a worthwhile force. For it will bring upset only if a life gives only to upset and one that is directed to a life of criticism can only criticise.

Let it be that you realise that by giving our love we create a nicer and worthwhile way forward. And that brings calm.

If we are fraught and the way forth is upsetting and anguished, it will bring more anguish and that is the setting to be avoided, for a better way is at hand and it will only benefit you to use it, for you are in favour of good.

Let it be that you simulate anger not, but give yourself to re-routing language and upset that is bound to unfold in your life, and allow them no time lost, but a need to generate good and worth, so that you can formulate a better way forward.

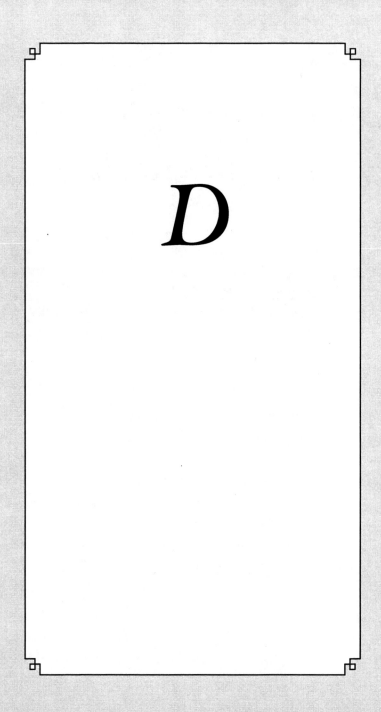

D

Death Part One
(Channelled 23 May 2007)

Key Points

- The need to die upsets many people but it is necessary to move on and graduate to a new level of worth.
- Some want to increase life by 5, 10 or even more years.
- It is impossible to treat everyone individually. They are to move on and die again many times in future lives.
- There is a transition period in spirit.
- Some people's timing is accurate. It is good they recognise that delay impedes their growth.
- Delaying past the time allowed can cause people suffering in their actual passing.
- Death is only a passing blow to the person you knew. They rise again in spirit form until there is a need for a new life on earth.

- Death is not a failure of life but the need for another life learning new abilities.
- Angels do not take you across. Many, who are known to you, help you.
- Any pain experienced in the human form, ends when the time arrives and the need to move on is accepted.
- Before they actually live their life everyone chooses how they will die.
- You are allowed to die at a slightly later stage if it is necessary.
- You must be strong and understand that death must go on with a need to bring life.
- There are many lives to live.
- Some create themselves a longer, more arduous pathway of learning.
- God's character is seen in all who learn, particularly those moving on in great worth.
- The soul lives on and gains more knowledge than can be gathered on Earth.
- Understand that life is taken with love.
- Life is given to bring simple worth to your soul and life is taken so that it may be well formulated for a later life.

A Clear Account

Jesus says that death baffles many people. It generally upsets them, and yet, he explains it is worthwhile for us all to die at some point so that we can move on and progress to the next level of learning.

Nevertheless, some people have a desire to live forever; they want to extend their life by five, ten or more years. As individuals we cannot do this; we have to continue our learning for the future and die again and again, and that must be fulfilled if we are to carry on in spirit form between our Earthly lives.

Some are actually precise in their timing and they are to be praised for this because they can see how a delay can only impede their growth. But others cannot see how it will cause them problems.

No one benefits from staying beyond the allowed time in fact they will suffer if they obstruct the course.

You should understand that death is only a passing blow to the person you once knew. They rise again in spirit form until there is a need for them to return to Earth on another mission. However, this passing blow is not a failure in the system of life instead it is a need to move forward to another life. And it brings with it a need to learn more abilities and to adjust to what has passed and be satisfied with it.

There are no angels to take you across, but there are many whom you knew, and they help you through the transition from pain and hardship in your human form to a renewed and able future. Because there is pain in our human form until we accept that the time has come and we must answer it.

But the truth is that everyone is able to move on in a way of their choosing, and that choice is made before they embark on this life and when they decide the type of life they need.

You cannot be resolute if you feel you cannot rearrange the time of your death, but there is some leeway here. The one thing you cannot change is how you will die as you have already chosen that. A short extension of time can be arranged if necessary. But it is only short.

You must understand that you have to be strong as the need for death will carry on but this creates a need for new life. For there are many lives to live and that will bring great knowledge and worth to some while others will not gain as much, for they will opt out where they see no need to take part, so they will create themselves a longer more arduous pathway of learning.

Understand too that God's character can be seen in all who learn, but the greatest facet is visible in those who act within their stage of life, and adjust so that they can move on in great acclaim. And because of the good they are given, they understand more and give more to life and they enjoy that which reflects God's principles.

Death is a passing and the soul lives on and learns more than it can on Earth. But it is given purpose, wisdom and life beyond imagination so that it can return again rich in character to learn again.

Focus on the fact that that which is given to you is taken with love, and that it will bring worth in life for just as the one we crave is taken it is formatted so that it is worthwhile to a later life, when knowledge is restored to live again in God's Love.

You should not let death upset you or anger you. Let it make you think differently about your life, for life can be over in a minute, or it can be longer. And it is that adjustment that allows us the need to live properly and fully in God's mercy.

The Writing

It is needed now to talk about the subject that baffles many people and that is the subject of death. For the need to die brings many people upset on a big scale and that cannot be, for it is of worth to us all to die at some point so that we can move on and graduate to the next level of worth.

But that needed by some is to live forever and they are not content with the time given to them but want an extra five years or ten years or more.

Yet that is impossible if we are to treat the person as an individual case. For they are to merit the need to follow on their learning with a skill held to future needs, and that is to die again and again in their future lives. For they will not die once but several times, and that must be fulfilled if they are to carry on the transitional pathway that awaits in spirit form.

For that given to some is to generate a way that is held to accurate timing and that must be applauded as they are correct and able to see that a manifested delay can only impede their growth, but there are others who are not so stable and they cannot see that they are generating upset by a need to stay longer than is necessary.

For it is fortuitous not to stay beyond that time that is given, for it is an upset to the bounds of time allowed for that person to die, and they will suffer as a result in the passing of obstructed worth.

Let it be that you know now that death is but a passing blow to the character of the person that you once knew, and they rise again in the life of spirit form until they are aware once again of a need to return to Earth as a person held to a mission.

But that force of death is only a passing blow, because it brings not failure to the system of life, but a need to be of worth to another life. And it brings with it a need to learn more abilities and to bring to life a need for adjustment and satisfaction in that past.

For there are no angels to bring you across at the end, but there are many who attend that are known to you, and help you in your need not to succumb to pain and hardship, but instead to a time of renewed life and ability.

For it is not without pain when we are in the human form until that time when we accept that the time is come and the need must be answered.

But if the truth is to be learnt it will be known that everyone is capable of moving on in the capacity of worth needed to fulfil a way of options. And so that brings unto them a choice of ways to die and that is to be decided at a time before that life is lived. And it is at that time that you choose in which way you are to die, just as you chose to be of one life or another. And that cannot bring a resolution if it is felt that you can rearrange not your time of death. But you can to a certain extent and that is offered to you. But you cannot choose by what method you die if you have already chosen, and that will not alter.

But if you need to die at a later stage and not when called it is made available to you to do this. But when the time has come, it is only within a short time that you have available that it can change and allow that of need to happen.

Let it be that you understand that a need shows now to be of stalwart character for the need to generate death must go on, but that of need is to bring life and not just death to the world and there will be a formatting of a new life as soon as that need shows to be of worth to creating one.

For there are many lives to be lived and that will bring great knowledge and worth to some people and less so to others, for they will feel that they need not partake in a willing state that holds no new need for them. And they will opt out of doing that which others do readily, and they will create for themselves a longer and more arduous pathway of learning.

Let it be that you learn soon that God's character may be seen in all who learn. But that of the greatest facet is to be seen in those who act within their stage of life and bring forth changes necessary to their being; that they may move on in tumultuous worth. And given that which is of service to good, enables them to understand more and give more to life, and enjoy that which is of wisdom to God's principles.

Let it be that you learn now that death is only a passing and no more, for the soul lives on and is wise in the learning of more than can be accumulated on Earth. But it is given purpose and life and a wisdom beyond all scope so that the need to return shall be given in fullness of character; that it may satisfy the need for information and learning.

Let it be soon that you adjust your lives to believe that that which is given to you is taken with love. And that that given is to bring you solace of worth in life, just as the life for which we crave must be taken and formatted to be of worth to a later life when all that is learned shall be restored and given to live again and fully in the knowing of God's Love.

Let it be you understand fully the concept of death, and that it does not anger or upset you, but gives you a need to think differently about life, for we are able to live a life within a minute or within a longer period until it is time to go. And it will be that adjustment that brings us the need to live properly and fully in God's mercy.

Death Part Two
(Channelled 24 May 2007)

Key Points

- It is necessary to describe the transient period between life and death, to allay fears and upset.
- Some pray for God's guidance and receive purpose and worth.
- Some will not pray and are often alone and misled in their actions.
- For some people a violent death provides a worthwhile exit from their time on Earth.
- There are no accidents in life. Each and every death is pre-planned unless someone suddenly takes their own life or someone else's.
- Those who murder will be redeemed and given help to reawaken the good within and heal the soul..
- Those who murder, rape etc., are given sanctity to remedy what is wrong.

- God's formula brings life within a minute or two of dying and then they arrive at the gate they need.
- The choice of a good or bad life follows through to death.
- Some wrongly believe the body sheds life when it cannot support it. In fact life leaves the brain first and the soul moves on to the spirit realm.
- Those who care about us meet us in the spirit realms.
- Although a death may bring grief to some on Earth there is happiness in the spirit realm.
- Death creates life. A life is born again to spirit for each body burned or buried.
- Each passing has been planned and is worthwhile.
- Premeditated murder or upset causes justifiable anger.
- God's principles allow for the taking of a life if it is according to God's laws.
- Those who commit murder that is not premeditated are not given the same sanctity.
- The need to be bad is given so that the world experiences all factors of good and evil.
- God needs some to be evil to bring about change in an upset world. A killing can prompt law changes.
- Do not assume a character to be bad if they have evil intent. They will only commit evil if there

is a need and that is to prompt changes in laws and accepted ways.

- God needs people to understand they choose their own way before embarking on life.
- All who believe in the Father are given the necessary sanctity. Some do not believe but if they are given the opportunity to do so and comply they are saved.
- God's worth is with every one whether or not they have brought repulsion through their acts.
- God brings justice, and those alienated by Godless acts will not suffer incriminations through a lifetime of upset, but by realising their mistakes and learning to create general peace and worth in their lives.

A Clear Account

Jesus says here that it is necessary to talk about the transient period between life and death so that those who have failing health are ready for what happens and will not be upset. At this stage some pray for God's guidance and this is good because it brings purpose and worth.

Some will not pray, so they are alone in their thoughts and may be misled in the way they act if they fail to understand. For it is necessary to formulate a simple way which will transform them in whatever way is needed.

If they are involved in a crime or a violent event it may not be simple to plan, but it is easy to live, as it gives them a worthwhile exit to their life on earth. And that may not be a premeditated death. It may be a sudden accident, but having said that, there are no real accidents in life. Each and every death is pre-planned unless it is someone's sudden decision to take their own life or someone else's.

Generations have paid the price of taking a life and upsetting the community. They will be redeemed as they need to progress, and they will be given the help necessary to re-awaken the good in them and make the soul well again.

Do not be surprised that those who murder or rape or commit similar crimes will be given the sanctity allowed to remedy what is wrong within them. They can then pass on to fuller more positive pursuits that allow them to grow better and more worthwhile.

You should now know the difference between good and bad and feel a need to change so that you are good within. You must understand that we can take someone from their transient state and bring immediate change. For God's formula is to bring life within a person within a minute or two, and it is then that they arrive at the gate they need, for they are given the choice in life to be good or bad and this may deem it necessary to follow this through to death.

Some places still hold the original belief that death means the body cannot support life any longer and it sheds it. This is not true, for the brain brings about change so that a wonderfully enduring future is given to the failing person. The body does not die until after life has left the brain and the soul has moved on to the spirit realm.

You must understand that we are all met by those in the spirit realms who love and care for us and although many suffer grief at the death of a loved one, happiness prevails as we arrive in the spirit realms. So what is of sadness to one is of glad heart to another.

The future provides opportunity to learn and it cannot be upsetting if it creates life, which it will. For one born again to a life in spirit accounts for each body burned or buried.

And that benefits everyone who is upset at the passing of a loved one for they know it is a happy and peaceful passing once the human form has been shed.

Those who mourn must know that mourning should not bring a dark cloud over everyone, for the passing has been planned and it is worthwhile to each one. Yet some feel anger at the pre-meditated murder and upset. This is not wrong for some suffer murder in the interchange of life that cannot be pre-meditated, but some anger is felt by people because of the planning and obstruction to justice.

You must understand that people are allowed to serve God's principles if they were given the task of taking a life so it was right to do this according to God's laws. But where there are those who are not pre-meditated they cannot be given the same sanctity.

For the need to be bad is given so that the world will experience all factors of good and evil. And if a person is to experience evil it will be worthwhile to them if they are murdered by one who has chosen to perform the act.

God does need some people to be evil, for it brings change in a world of upset. And if it is necessary to kill it may verify and instigate a change in the law so that humanity's needs are appreciated.

Do not assume someone's character to be bad if they have evil intent, for it will only bring evil if it is given a need and then only to prompt changes in laws and accepted ways.

Understand now that there are many sanctions on life and being worthwhile so it is of greatest importance.

So it is necessary for some to understand that God's attitude is to ensure that people realise they choose their own way by making these important decisions before embarking on their life.

Here Jesus states that all who believe in the Father are given sanctity according to their need. But some people do not believe in God however they will be saved if they take the opportunity of learning to believe and then keep to it.

God's worth remains with each individual whether they have repulsed others through their act or generated faith.

God brings justice and those alienated by Godless acts shall not suffer recriminations through a lifetime of upset but by realising their mistakes and following a need to generate peace and worth in their lives.

The Writing

It is necessary now to talk of the transience between life and death, for that needs to be told so that those who are aware of failing health may not be upset or unready for the action taken.

When a person is failing in health they are often struck by the need to pray for God's guidance and this is good, for it formats a way forward of purpose and worth.

Let it be known that there are also those who will not pray, and they are alone in their thoughts and misled in their actions, if they are unable to fathom that which is given.

For it is necessary to bring to a person of need a way forth that is simple and able to transform them to their needed way forward. And that may not be simple to plan if they are involved in crime or in a way necessary to bring about a violent way forward. But it is actually easy for the ones of need to perform in life, as it gives them a way out that is worthwhile to their career here on Earth. And that may not be premeditated death but an accident that is to happen suddenly.

Let it be that you understand that there are no accidents in life, but that each and every act of death is preplanned unless the need shows to be of obvious worth to someone to take a life that is theirs or not theirs in the planning.

Let it be that you understand now that there are generations of people who have paid the price of upsetting the community through a death. And they shall be redeemed as they need to progress, and they will be given that help necessary to format a re-awakening of the good within them, and a formula given to substitute good in the soul so that it is well again.

Let it be that you are not astonished to learn that those who murder or rape or bring about a medley of upsetting worths, shall be given the sanctity allowed, that they may remedy the wrong within them and pass on to fuller and more willing pursuits that allow them to grow better and more worthwhile as people.

Let it be that you are now able to discern between good and bad and are given that need to change within your life that which is bad, and become good within.

Let it be that you know that we are able to take a person from their transient state and bring about change immediately. For that of the format of God's creation is to bring life within a person within a minute or two, and it is then that they arrive at the gate of their need, for they are given the choice in life to be good or bad, and that may deem the necessity of following the pathway through to death.

For it is of original belief in some places still that the body cannot support the life any further and it is given the need to shed life within. But it is not true for the format of the brain brings about change so that a way forward is given that is of magnificent endurance towards the failing person. And it is allowed that the body dies not until after the life has left the brain and the spirit met with its new capacity for worth within the spirit realm.

Let it be that you understand that we are all met by those who love and care for us, and we understand that the way of grief may come to many who suffer at the death of a loved one. But happiness prevails in the realms of spirit, and that which is of sadness to one is of glad heart to another.

For the way forth provides a way that is of great value to the need to learn, and the attitude is given worth to a need that the way forth cannot be of upset if it creates life and it shall create life, for one born again to a life in spirit is of worth to each body buried or burned. And that shall be of merit to all those who are upset at the passing of a loved one, for they are assured of a happy and peaceful passing once that of the human form has been shed.

Let it be that you understand that a need remains for some to mourn for their parent or loved one, but this is not so in all cases. For the worth is shown not to be of upset to some. But the need to mourn must not bring a dark cloud over each person held to it for they are mourning a passing that has been planned and been of purpose to a person.

Yet there are some who are unable to contain their anger when there is a pre-planned murder or upset. And this is not misplaced. For there are those who are able to suffer murder in the interchange of life that cannot be pre-meditated, but there are those too who anger some by their planning and their obstruction to justice.

Let it be that you know now that these people are allowed to be of service to God's principles if they are given a task that relates to the taking of a life, and it is given that they are right to do this in the upholding of God's laws, where some are of errant behaviour and may suffer the act of murder performed. But there are those who are premeditated not and they cannot be given the same sanctity of worth.

For that need to be bad is given that the world shall experience all factors of good and evil. And if a person is to experience evil it will be worthwhile to them if they are killed in a murderous fashion by one who is elected to perform the act.

Let it be that you know now that God needs not all to be evil but some, for the need shows to bring about change in a world of upset. And if that given is to kill, it will then bring about a change in the law and appreciation of humanity's needs to verify the need for change.

Let it be that you assume not the character to be bad that is of evil intent. For it will not bring evil unless it is given a need, and then only to change laws and accepted ways forward.

Let that of your need now hold to understanding that there are many sanctions made on life and that to be worthwhile to life is of greatest importance. It is therefore necessary to show some that the attitude of God is to impress on people that they determine their way forward by choosing that of importance before life begins.

And it is now that I say to you that all who believe in the Father are given sanctity of worth to their need. But there are some who do not believe and they will be saved if they format a way of greatest need where someone is given the way of opportunity and then given the need to comply.

Let it be you understand that the worth of God remains with each one whether they have repelled others through their act or given a need to generate faith.

Let it be so that you realise that God brings justice and those alienated by Godless acts shall suffer recriminations not by enduring a lifetime of upset, but by realising where they have gone wrong and attending to a need to generate sanctity and worth to their lives.

Divine Love (Channelled 16 May 2007)

Key Points

- Divine love is more fulfilling than anything known to the Human Race.
- When a need shows then God's love is given.
- God's wish for you to give out love must be upheld even when you get nothing in return.
- Trust and respect is all about loving people.
- If we love others we give them the need to create the same. They will change if they are committed to value.
- This will bring great happiness and a need to look for the good in life and not the bad.

A Clear Account

Jesus says here that there is a divine love and it is more fulfilling than anything known to the Human Race. For God's love is given when the need is there and if we have purpose and direction, that means always.

God's purpose is fulfilled when everyone has a need to serve Him and bring that level of appreciation and respect to their lives that is worthwhile and good.

God's wishes must be upheld. Sometimes that means giving out love when you know you will not receive anything in return.

Bringing trust and respect to everyone is just a matter of love, but until we find the need to do that we will not enjoy the fulfilment of God's love, for as we give love to people we give them a need to also create love that is good. Because you are just one person and there are many more in the picture who will make changes and be worthwhile if they are given the commitment and value needed.

So be determined and make that essential change that allows you to act with love in whatever way is needed so that you follow God's Laws and love everyone.

It will bring untold happiness if you do this and it will give you a need to look for the good in life, and not the bad.

The Writing

It is true that there is a Love Divine, and it is fulfilling beyond all that is known to man, for the fulfilment of God's Love is given when a need is shown, and that shall be always if we are given purpose and direction in our lives.

For that fulfilment of God's purpose shall bring to everyone a need to serve God and bring that worship to their lives that is necessary and good.

Let it be that you know now that God's wishes must be upheld, and if that means to give love when fulfilment cannot be seen, let it be that you do, for that need to bring faith and worship to all people is about love, and it shall not be until we can find and fulfil that need that we shall enjoy the fulfilment of God's Love in that time.

For we are then giving all people a need to generate the love we feel, and that is good. For you are but one in the picture and there are many more who will fulfil and bring about the changes necessary to their lives if they are given commitment and worth.

Let your attitude be to bring about the change necessary and then to act in love wherever and however it is needed, so the need shall become great to act within God's Laws and to love everyone.

Let it be soon that this happens for it will bring happiness untold and a great need to live for the good in life and not bad

Dreams (Channelled 10 May 2007)

Key Points

- Messages sometimes come in dreams to help you to be positive about things.
- If you are depressed or anxious, this can carry through to your dreams.
- Dreams can show adjustments to your pathway that will bring satisfaction and worth.
- An upsetting task can bring an upsetting dream, but if you dream it you can accomplish what you need.
- Images are given by the brain unless it is clearly relating to God's pathway.
- The message within your dream is the most helpful part and it formulates in such a way that you can feel optimistic or upset.

A Clear Account

Jesus says that you sometimes receive messages in your dreams. Maybe they will show you a way of success so that you stay positive, but if you are depressed or anxious this can also carry to your dreams.

During sleep, you are given an understanding of what can happen during a period of time. It is something you can expand on and live. It can not only show the original formula of your pathway but also bring an adjusted formula, which can add to your satisfaction and worth.

If it is something upsetting you have to do, you may feel troubled, but if you dream it you will accomplish your task.

Uplifting dreams can bring hope and a need to live a fulfilling life. The images are given by the brain unless God's pathway requires that different ones are seen. But the message is more helpful than the image itself. It will help you to feel optimistic or upset.

The Writing

You can sometimes receive messages through your dreams. They are there to encourage you to take a positive approach to things.

If you are depressed or anxious, what you feel can carry to your dreams, so that you experience the reaction to your feelings. However if you are happy and positive about the future it can be very different, because while you are asleep you are given an understanding of what can happen within a certain time span.

It's a formula that you can then expand and live. Not only will you live that which is preordained, but circumstances may bring changes that leave you feeling even more satisfied and worthwhile.

If there is something upsetting that you have to experience you will feel that, but you will achieve a better result if you have received it in a dream. Upsetting dreams can pull you down, but if the dream is uplifting and makes you feel positive it will bring hope and generate within you a need for fulfilment.

Your brain devises the images you see, unless you need to be shown something that particularly points to God's pathway.

It is the message that is held within the dream that is important to you, rather than the pictures you see. The message will formulate in whatever way is necessary to carry over to you a feeling of upset or a feeling of optimism.

Drugs (Channelled 20 June 2007)

Key Points

- Many people are addicted to drugs in order to suppress fear and enjoy a release from obligations in their lives.
- It is a serious situation.
- Without so much pressure and stress, fewer people would take drugs. Stresses start in childhood.
- There is a need to encourage good behaviour in the young.
- It is necessary to allow less freedom to do upsetting things.
- Young people are not guided in many families.
- Young people are condemned rather than supported.
- Some reformed addicts help others to change and that is good, but it is not enough to do this as by then the addiction exists.
- There is need to provide more reform groups in schools.

- Help people to learn not to partake in drugs.
- Pray for those affected by drugs so that it instigates change.
- Bring families closer so that they face problems together, and do not alienate family members with the result that they start drugs.

A Clear Account

Many people are addicted to drugs because they want to suppress their fears and escape obligations for a time. More and more are succumbing and it is very serious because there is no cure, only treatment for the symptoms.

Yet many would not take drugs if there were less stress and pressure in their lives. Many of these stresses begin in childhood and are established enough that addiction becomes the route later on.

You must understand that there is a need to improve the behaviour of the young and give them less freedom to do distressing things, because at the moment they are not given guidance in many families so they join others and put right their ills in that way. They are condemned instead of being supported and that outlook will not change things for the better.

It is good to see some reformed addicts helping others to change, but that is not enough because the addiction exists by then.

There should be more reform groups in schools and support for the ones who have learned that drugs are bad and claim many lives.

You need to generate faith in God's Word and pray for changes to begin. You also need to bring families closer so that they are united in the face of problems and do not alienate the ones who need support. In that way they will not break away and join those who take drugs.

The Writing

There are numbers of people in the world who are addicted to drugs to support fear and enjoy the delight of release from all obligations within a time.

There are more and more who are succumbing and it is very serious. It is addictive behaviour that is the groundswell and there is no cure for it but to treat that of the symptoms.

Yet many would not take the pathway of drugs if there were not so much stress and pressure in their lives, for there are many stresses that arise in childhood and are formulated sufficiently to bring about addiction later.

Let it be that you understand now a need to generate good behaviour among the young and to bring them a need to adjust their lives so that they are given less freedom to bring about upset in their lives. For they are given not guidance in many families and their need is to join with others in the need to rectify ills within

their lives, for they are given not support, but condemnation and that attitude will not bring about changes
for the better.

It is good to see that some reformed addicts help
others to change, but it is not enough and by then the
addiction exists.

Let it be that there are more reform groups within
schools and a generating of worth towards the ones who
have learned that it is good not to partake in the cruel
addiction that claims so many lives. Let it be that you
adjust now to a need to generate faith in God's Word
and bring about a clemency of time when all who are
of need are prayed for, and that will instigate steps to
bring about change.

Let it be also that you bring about changes within
families that allow them to bring together that family
approach towards problems and not alienate the ones
who need support so that they are ready to break away
with those of need unto drugs.

E

Enjoy Your Life
(Channelled 12 May 2007)

Key Points

- Do you feel obliged to make money and forget the need to enjoy life?
- Bring God's virtue to your work and you will feel the benefit, doing what is right for your life and not just generating money.
- Forget the lavish life, instead feel total wellbeing.
- Be worthwhile to God's purpose and improve your life by not always earning money, but instead spending time helping others.
- Value yourself more and not just money.
- You will feel more worthwhile if you serve God's values instead.

A Clear Account

In this writing Jesus asks you a direct question. Do you really enjoy life or is it a case that you feel obliged to earn more and more money and miss out on your life?

It is good to enjoy your life, and if you focus on it you will do so, for by bringing in God's virtue on how you work you will benefit from doing what is right for your life – and not just making money.

You can have a really enjoyable life if you are able to realise that by settling for a less lavish lifestyle and living more to God's purpose you will achieve it. By realising God's values, and by valuing yourself and not just money, you will be better able to divide your resources so that others can benefit too. And this will make you feel worthwhile, and you will be tempted less materially and serve God's values instead.

You will find personal satisfaction and you will be much happier as you grow as a person. Try to realise that this is the way forward and immediately the future will be of great benefit.

The Writing

Do you enjoy your life? Do you feel obligated to fulfil a need to generate money and forget the need to enjoy life too?

It is good to enjoy your life and you will more, if you dedicate yourself to it.

For it is by bringing God's virtue to the work that you will feel the benefit of doing what is right for your life, and not just what is given to be worthwhile to generating money, but it will bring you a better life if you can allow yourself to settle for a lavish life not, but generate a better worth instead.

Let it be that you are worthwhile to God's purpose, and bring yourself a better life, by generating that which obligates you not to accumulate money, but divide your resources between others' needs too so that they can benefit also.

Let it be that you hold a need to give yourself more value and not just more money, for it will bring you satisfaction and worth in your life, for it will bring you a need to generate worth by yielding to temptation less and holding a need to serve God's values instead. It will bring you satisfaction and worth in your life and you will be ecstatic as you grow as a person.

Let it be soon that you realise this, for the way forward will be of great benefit as soon as you do.

Evil (Channelled 18 June 2007)

Key Points

- You need to adjust your life so you avoid evil.

- Evil is a great force. People must not be swept away uncontrollably by it.

- You must be strong against evil. It will win where it can. Only a greater force of good can overcome it.

- There are many situations where evil is seen. Avoiding these brings a clear mind and value to your day.

- You are bound by God's Power. He guides you and helps you to avoid what is bad.

- Everyone has an evil streak which will show if needed.

- Everyone must understand that they have the choice of being good or evil, and they will fulfil that as they need.

- There are many more places that are evil both in their value and their intent, so all who can do so must follow a good life rather than evil.

A Clear Account

Jesus says here that it is necessary to adjust your life to avoid evil for its strength is great and all people need to ensure they are unlikely to be swept away in an evil frenzy over which they have not control.

You must understand that you have to be strong in the face of evil. It is a force that will win if it can and unless the force of good is stronger, it will not abate. You need to avoid evil situations in your life. There are many of them and if you avoid them it will be worthwhile to your day, and bring you a clear mind. For you are bound by God's power. He guides you and He will make you feel valued enough that you will not focus on the bad.

However, everyone has an evil streak and it will show if they need it to. So it is necessary to tell people that information which is necessary for them to bring about trust and wise choices.

All people have a choice to be good or evil, and they will fulfil that in whichever way is needed. But there are many more places that are of mal intent and value evil. Because of this we need to ensure that everyone who needs to moves their focus away from evil and creates good.

The Writing

It is necessary to adjust life's pattern so that it encounters not evil, for the force of evil is very great and that need now is to bring unto all people a need to adjust their lives so that they are less likely to be swept away in an evil frenzy, of which they have not control.

Let it be that you understand a need to be of substantial force against evil. For it will win where it can and it will not abate, unless the force of good is seen to be of greater worth unto it.

Let it be you understand now a need to bring forth wisdom that can enable you to avoid the situation where evil is seen. For there are many and it will be an aversion to this that can bring clarity of thought and worth to your day.

For you are bound by God's power. He is there to guide you and He will bring you all the worth necessary to avert your gaze from that which is bad, but where the need is, there is an evil streak in all people and they will respond to it if given the need to.

It is therefore necessary now to bring all people to the point of trust and wisdom that that given may be read and fully understood.

For the need is to bring unto all people an option to be good or evil, and that will bring them a need to serve in whatever way they can, but there are many more institutions where there is evil intent and worth, and that of the need shall bring forth a change to their character and be of worth to goodness rather than evil.

Food for the Soul
(Channelled 10 May 2007)

Key Points

- We are given feelings to experience so that we can judge between right and wrong.
- Challenges are a more rewarding experience because we have feelings.
- To benefit fully from challenges they cannot be attempted coldly and mechanically.
- It is a combination of mind, body and spirit that experiences life.
- Integrate positive experiences into your day to escape the distress many feel.
- Aim for a combined benefit.

A Clear Account

Jesus says here that that which affects the body and the mind is easily seen but even though the spirit is as much of a priority, effects on the feelings can be less evident.

It is good we have feelings. Life would not be good without them. They are there to help us judge right from wrong and they allow us to enjoy both emotions of comfort and of sadness.

Feelings are as important to our lives as nourishment is to a child. Challenges are better for the feelings we experience when we face them. They cannot be done coldly, mechanically.

To find fulfilment in achieving our goals we must have the benefit of feelings. They are part of the total wellbeing of a person and are to be nourished just as we feed the mind and the body. They cannot be ignored 95% of the time, and brought out at special times. It is a whole picture.

Learn to integrate a positive experience into your day to avoid the distress others may endure, be aware and never isolate areas of your being. Achieve total wellbeing.

The Writing

Jesus tells us that it is important to learn that which involves the body and mind can be seen to have an effect, but that which involves the spirit affects only the feelings which are as important, but are not readily seen.

For it is fortuitous that we have feelings for without them it would be a time of misfortune, for we are given those feelings to experience, so that we may judge between right and wrong. And to give that which is important in our lives a need to give forth a feeling of comfort, while our upsets can be felt by a need to cry and to share sadness.

Let it be that you know that the feelings felt by one, are as able to procure worth to our life as the need to succour a child is to bring life.

Let it be that you understand now that a way of challenges shall be better fed if it has the importance of feelings attached. For they cannot be coldly held apart from the rigours of life and left to live alone in the accomplishment of worth attached to a particular experience.

For it must be lived alongside the need to generate worth to the brain and to the body's needs to survive., for it is a combined force that brings life as it should be lived, and not a separate worth which is held to only at special times, and is ignored for the rest of the time.

Let it be that you learn now to integrate into your day a feeling of positive experience, so that you may give yourself a release from the upsets that cause unrest among others.

Let it be that you are vigilant and give all to achieve that of a combined power and not one of isolation.

Formula of Love
(Channelled 8 June 2007)

Key Points

- Man is selfish in many ways.
- Past happenings have led people to believe there is no God, which has resulted in Godless behaviour.
- God is present at all times.
- You have the ability to communicate love to everyone.
- Choose a way of love not contempt.
- Many ways can cause havoc and hate but they dull lives and upset people.
- You should formulate a way of kindness and love so that the way of the Lord can be seen.
- Bring about changes to formulate benefit and not grief or obstruction to good.

A Clear Account

Jesus says that man is selfish in many ways and it is necessary to bring goodness and not contempt in the world. Because of past factors many believe there is no God and therefore that has brought about Godlessness and upset.

Yet there are many areas where God has made you feel good. You are able to communicate with others in many ways and have the ability to link with them in love. You may doubt this and so you will not feel His presence, but He is always with you to help you discover an exciting and worthwhile life.

You are able to give out love and encourage everyone on the planet to do the same, and that is what God wants. So choose a loving life rather than a contemptuous one, for there are many that follow God's needs. There are also many ways to cause havoc and hate but resist these because they only hurt and upset people.

Choose one of the many loving ways. Find a formula to suit you and one that shows the teaching of the Lord and the benefit of obeying God's rules. In fact, change your life so that you bring about good rather than obstruct it.

The Writing

It is necessary today to talk of the way man behaves towards others, for he is a selfish character in many ways, and that need now is to bring about a change so that that which is of goodness is seen within and not contempt.

For the way past has led many people to believe there is no God, and there has been an evaluating of that factor that has brought about Godlessness and upset as a result.

Forthwith let there be an accurate assumption of God's presence held, for there are many factors in which he is present, for He has given to you a need to formulate good in your life, and you will be given an accurate description of this if you read on, for there are many areas where God has given you worth. He has given you an ability to communicate with others in whatever way. He has given you an ability to link with others in love and communication and He has brought forth a need in you to communicate this love to others, for He has given to you so that you do this and yet you may not have believed this to be true; for you have been unaware of His presence.

And yet He is there at all times to serve a need not to embellish your life with all things dull and uninteresting, but in a way that is exciting and worthwhile, for you are able to communicate with all people on this planet and bring to them a need to serve that which is of God's choice too and that is love.

Let it be that you do this for you are worthy of choice and so let it be that you choose a way of love and not contempt, for there are ways abundant to the need of God, but there are many also that cause havoc and hate, and they must be fought against and put down so that they may never again dull lives and upset. For there are many ways to please God's way and there are many versions that can adopt a pattern of love if they are given that chance.

Let it be your need now to formulate a way of kindness and love so that the way of the Lord may be seen to be of tumultuous worth in the way forth, and bring unto all people a need to serve God in the obeying of His rules.

Let it be so that you bring about changes to your life that will formulate benefit and not grief or obstruction to the way of good.

Fulfilment (Channelled 10 May 2007)

Key Points

- Feel fulfilled and it will enhance your life so much that you will want to achieve more and generate even greater feelings of good.
- Your mission is to be happy within the framework of your life.
- New purchases do not bring the same values as God given pleasures.
- Simplicity brings a feeling of being worthwhile.
- Recent priorities have turned towards purchases bought through loans and the values of God have been harmed by it.
- The human race cannot live by debt and excess spending.
- Time cannot be spent defacing parts of the world to make money and feeding short term gain.
- The worth of God is there to bring substance and worth to your life. Be proud of this.

A Clear Account

Jesus says here that feeling fulfilled will give you such a value that you will feel you have to achieve more, bring more to your life and prolong your feeling of ecstasy.

For your mission is to be happy within the framework of your life. Concentrate on formulating a future that brings you fulfilment. It will not be found when you purchase a new house, but in simple God given pleasures like a walk.

It is necessary to live a simple life and when you achieve that, you find the philosophy is very meaningful. For God's worth is better and wiser than anything that man can come up with in a life time.

In recent times confidence has been harmed in God's importance, and priority has been given to having things like a large car and an even larger bank loan to support it.

The formula for life cannot be achieved this way. The human race cannot use its time on Earth running up debt and spending excessively. The time is precious and must be spent appreciating what is in the world and not defacing parts of it with buildings in order to get money. This will only bring a short term thrill.

You have to understand soon that God's worth is there to bring you substance and meaning. Be proud of this.

The Writing

Feel fulfilled and it will magnify your worth to such an extent that you will feel a need to achieve more, to bring more to your life and to hold a need that brings you ecstatic feelings that are prolonged.

For you are given a mission in life and that is to be happy within the framework you are living.

Let it be that you give all your need to formulating a future that can bring you fulfilment. For it will not be found when you are handling all the paperwork for the purchase of a new house, but it will be found if you bring yourself to enjoy a walk or some other simple pleasure that is God given.

For the need is to live a simple life and if that can be achieved, it will bring you a philosophy that is very worthwhile, and that is that God's worth is better and wiser than all the man made issues that are given in a life time.

For the building of confidence in God's worth has been harmed in recent times as things that are of priority have been a large bank statement, a large car and an even larger bank loan to support it all

It cannot be that the formula for life can be avoided in this way. It cannot be that man's time on Earth is taken up by debt and excess spending, for his time on Earth is of exceptional worth and his time must be spent in realising the worth of all that is around him, and not the defacing of one site to build another building that is not meant but for the making of money, and a dismal approach to finance that makes everything you sought seem worthwhile for a short time only.

Let it be soon you realise that the worth of God is to bring you substance and worth to your life, and let that be an accomplishment of which you are proud.

G

Generate Goodness (Channelled 21 June 2007)

Key Points

- People are free to choose goodness and worth, but pick resentment and hate.
- There is a need to change as resentment brings cruelty, not love.
- God needs to communicate with love.
- Some bring hate to mankind.
- Resolve to generate goodness.
- Goodness brings more harmony to the world.
- God's love will endow you with great qualities for the future.
- This will power you on to succeed.
- Start soon.

A Clear Account

Jesus says that many have the freedom to choose goodness and worth in their lives, but they opt for hate and resentment instead.

There is a need for you to change because resentment brings cruelty and upset rather than love. God needs us to communicate with love in our hearts, but some choose to use a formula un-necessary to mankind, and that is hate.

Resolve to generate goodness so that it brings value to life and creates more harmony in the world. There is no middle man. God brings you the protection of love and the quality of that will bring great value to your future.

It will power you on to succeed, so start soon.

The Writing

It is necessary now to write on the freedom that people have in their lives to choose goodness and worth. But that of the need turns to hate and resentment whenever a need shows.

Let it be that you adjust your need to bring about change, for resentment brings cruelty and upset, and not the value of love.

For God's sake we are able to communicate with each other and bring love to our hearts, but that of the need to some is to bring hate in a formula unnecessary to mankind.

Let it be that you are resolute in your need to generate that goodness needed that formulates worth, for it brings far more harmony to the world. And that given must be between all who are of harmony to each other, for there is no middle man here. It is a protected feeling between God and you and it shall be that the level of love given, shall endow you with great qualities for the future.

Let it be so, for that will dynamise your need to succeed. Let it be soon that you start.

Gnomes (Channelled 11 June 2007)

Key Points

- In the world there are no dwarves or pixies but there are upsetting gnomes especially in areas where there is a lack of good.
- There used to be pixies and they were good. Some lied about their goodness and pixies' presence in the world ended. They now live and play elsewhere.
- Gnomes were discovered and named many years before God created man as he is today.
- Some feel God created a need to generate hate rather than fulfilment in the world.
- Godlessness ruled at one time. It was a time of great cruelty and hate.
- Gnomes existed from before the time of Christ.
- They are not taller than table height.
- Gnomes brought bad feeling and hate to the world because they were enveloped in greed and hate and had a bad effect on mankind, halting

his progress, affecting his health and his need to serve God.

- There is a need for good and evil in the world.
- Man is valued by his trust in God and in trusting that which is worthwhile around him.
- Fairies and angels bring good
- It is necessary to have a variety of elements in the world.
- Gnomes exist to aggravate and upset us and they generate evil wherever they can.
- They are virulent where there are elements of Godlessness. They cannot exist where God rules.
- There must be change.
- There is a diary kept by a man in the 18th century that confirms the existence of gnomes at a time of slavery and hardship for black races of people.
- Gnomes live and grow abundantly if they are allowed.
- Like the fairies they are not seen.
- Fairies bring enchantment and good to us if they are allowed.
- We can invoke the malice of gnomes.
- They cannot hurt us if we do not allow it, but the instant we do they live on and create more evil.
- We must rid the world of evil and create a balance towards goodness and worth to help those at risk.

- The force of gnomes exists and it will bring grief wherever it strikes in abundance.

A Clear Account

Jesus says that he needs to explain about the presence of gnomes in the world especially where good does not prevail. He says there are no dwarves or pixies although at one time pixie nations did inhabit the world. They did influence good but some people lied about them and said they brought trouble. So after a while pixies came to an end so that the fabric of the world could change and they moved to another place where they still play and bring luck and wisdom to those who need it.

But gnomes date back before the time of Christ. In fact they were discovered and named many years before God created man as he is today.

You have to understand that some believe that God created a need for hate in the world rather than fulfilment and good. At one time it was said that the way forward was to create hate but it was not true, however it symbolised a time when Godlessness ruled and was a time of great cruelty and trouble. It was around this time that gnomes were discovered. They were man like creatures but stood no taller than a table, however they brought malice and hate to the world. They were enveloped in greed and brought a bad effect to the human race, because its progress was halted as was the health of individuals and their need to serve God.

You must understand that there is a need for good and evil, for there are many things that judge the value of a person and obviously the need to trust in God is one. But there is also a need to trust that around them because not everything in the world is of value to mankind.

There is proof of the existence of gnomes within the diary of a man who lived in the 18th century when slavery and malice towards black people was rife.

Fairies and angels bring good and there is also a bad force to restore the equal and opposite force needed. God has many obligations to bring goodness and value to the world and a God like quality is a priority for the human race, but there are various elements that need to make up a world and provide the right formula for their needs.

Gnomes are there to disrupt and upset us whenever they can. They are there to generate bad and they do this wherever they can. Where there is a Godless rule in the world they are prevalent and now there is a need to lessen the power they hold. If God rules the world they cannot exist, but they can if they are given malice and trouble to live on.

The Writing

That of the need now is to explain that there are no dwarves or upsetting pixies in the world, but there are many of the more upsetting variety of gnomes held to areas of the world where there are virulent strains of abstinence to good. For there are areas of the world where there were once the pixie nations, and they brought forth change to good. And yet this was not recognised by some and there were fabrications made about the upset caused by pixies and they were not true, but they were virulent. And so a time came when all the pixies of the world came to an end through the need to adjust the fabric of the world, and they are now brought forth to another place where they play and are given that freedom to bring luck and wisdom to all those who need.

But there are others within the world that are malice made and they are the ones called not hobbits but gnomes, for they are given the name of gnome by the one who discovered them in the many years before God created man as he is today.

Let it be that you adjust your mind to the knowing that there are some who think that God created not worth in the world but a need to generate hate. For it was said at one time that a way stood forth to bring about a generation of hate within the world and that was not true. And yet it symbolised a time when Godlessness ruled and it was a time of great cruelty and upset.

It was at this time that there was discovered a race of manlike creatures that were there from before Christ and they were of upright stature but were so small they could not rise above a table height. Yet this race of creatures brought malice and hate to the world for they were enveloped in greed and upset and could not affect well the race of man within the world, for he was brought to a halt by the profound upset of the gnomes and they were affecting his need to be robust and well in his need to serve God. Yet there was more of a constraint among those who believed in good than those who believed in the badness of the world's needs at the time.

Let it be you understand the whole need for a force of good and evil. For there are many things that value a man and that of his need to trust in God is apparent, but there is also a need to generate trust in the abundant worth about him. For there are many values attached to the world and they are not all held to be of value to mankind. For there are fairies and the angels too that bring good and there must also be the element of bad to restore worth to the equal and opposite values needed to the world.

Let it be that you understand now that there are many obligations to God to provide worth to the world, and that must be evaluated as a priority that is of Godlike worth in mankind, but also there stands a need for those various elements that are to make up a world in the formula needed for mankind's needs.

Let it be you understand that the gnomes are to be there to aggravate and upset us at every turn, for they are there to generate bad and they will bring evil wherever they can. But their abundant growth has been seen where that of a Godless rule has abounded and that of the need is to eliminate some of the power held by them. They cannot exist if God is given rule over a world, but they can if they are given malice and upset to live upon.

Let it be that you know they are little creatures of upset and that need now is to bring about change where

there is malice and hold in the love of God for the fulfilment of all people. Let it be that you understand that all
this is true and there is verification of this within every
page of every diary kept by a man of worth in the eight-
eenth century, when there were many malice's held towards black men and those who were enslaved.

Let it be that you understand now that the gnome
is a living creature and it will abundantly grow where
it is allowed, but it is not seen and it is like the fairies in
that they disappear when a man may be held to enquire
about them but they reappear when needed.

For the force of good there is evil, and just as the
fairies bring good and enchantment to our lives as we
allow, we may also invoke the malice of gnomes. For
they are about us at every stage of life, but they cannot harm us or create evil if we do not allow it, but the
moment we allow them an entry into our hearts we are
giving them a need to live on and create more evil. So
we must invoke a need to rid the world of evil so that
we balance again that which is of goodness and worth
in the world, and bring about change in the way needed
to alleviate stress and upset in the lives of those most at
risk. Let it be soon you realise that this is a force within
the world that will not pass but will bring grief wherever it strikes in abundant force.

God Is With You
(Channelled 10 May 2007)

Key Points

- God's values encourage those who are aware to act thoughtfully.
- They grow closer to Him developing as they go.
- Everyone should serve God because they will appreciate more.
- It will prompt change and then more change.
- They will find fulfilment and that will encourage them to continue.
- They will begin to serve others
- God is with you all the time.
- Assess your life and realise God has a purpose within it.
- God is the proof of all that is worthwhile in your life and beyond.

A Clear Account

Jesus tells us that when people are aware, God's values bring them a need to act thoughtfully.

As they serve God, they grow closer to Him and feel His presence, and it is a lovely feeling living each day and developing as well.

It is time now for everyone to serve God because by doing so they will feel more appreciative and content. As they work in this way they will find changes that are so great that they will want to continue and change even more.

The formula will bring fulfilment which will in turn encourage them to experience even more, and instead of just following rules they will seek more duties including serving others.

You must understand that God is with you every day. In the same breath He will fulfil you and demand more of you.

Take a look at your life and see that God has a purpose within it. He will bless it as you serve His values and follow a blessed pathway.

Decide soon that your future is with God and not without Him, and that He is the proof of all that is really worthwhile in your life and beyond.

Do it soon.

The Writing

It is true that God's values are such that He shall bring to all people who hear a need to be circumspect in their dealings.

For they are to be worthwhile to God in their need to serve God's Pathway. And that shall bring them closer to God, so they feel His presence with them at all times. And that will bring them great pleasure as they attend to the needs of the day, and bring forth the changes necessary to their characters.

For that need now is to bring to all people a need to serve God, so they may feel fulfilled and worshipful in a way that brings them closer to God.

And that manipulation of their time shall bring a change so great that they will feel a need to follow on and bring about changes on a greater scale.

For that formula will bring fulfilment, and that fulfilment must bring them a need to serve a fuller and more willing experience; that it may even provide a need to serve God by generating worth among others, and contemplate the future as a whole being, seeking duty and not just one who is of observance to the rules.

Let it be soon that you are able to understand that God is with you each day and will fulfil you and obligate you at the same time in the same breath.

Let it be soon that you evaluate your life and say that God has a purpose within your life. And He shall be seen to be of virtue to your life as you pursue the way of all things blessed, and are felt to be of service to God's values.

Let it be soon that you determine that your future is with God and not without Him, and that He is the verification of all that is of true worth in your life and beyond. Let that be soon.

God's Work (Channelled 25 May 2007)

Key Points

- Our overriding attitude dictates the value within our lives
- Many have lost their need to do God's work because they are not happy with the message brought to them.
- Those who carried God's message to the people failed and left the order. They left the church in droves.
- God's values mean something and relate to modern life
- Mankind learned values that do not apply to living properly.
- The poor cannot relate to God's changed values when they see priests and clergy living comfortably and well.
- Many men would become priests except for the vow of celibacy. Why should they take that when they are young and need to have a family?

- Churches need to commit to areas of Africa where there is a need for Christianity, but the church opposes expenditure.
- No-one should train a person to believe in Christ if that is not their path. The heart must decide.
- Many in Africa need food and development.
- It is necessary to comply with God's worth. Fulfilment follows.
- People should no longer beg for food.
- It is necessary now to respect and follow God's rules.
- God's values mould the world so that worth is seen and built on. Start this and appreciate its value.

A Clear Account

Jesus says that it is our overriding attitude that dictates the value within our lives, because we are God's people and it is His attitude we bring to others. And yet there are many who are not resolved to do God's work. They would but they are not happy with the message that is brought to them.

Those whom God brought to Earth to resolutely carry His message to the people failed to do this and left the order. And so the message has not carried the worth of God since then.

They left the church in droves, and the need to follow God's character has left them distressed. For forthrightness has been abandoned and replaced with stupid and unreasonable decisions.

These values let down our friends. They must be released so that God's values actually mean something and relate to modern life.

The human race has in some ways been given free expression, learning values that do not apply to living properly.

God's priests and clergy should bring about change in the character of the people, but that has not happened. Yet while they live comfortably and well, they cannot see that the poor, with whom they sometimes work, cannot relate to God's changed values. For we can all call on God at times of need, and it is time that some of those priests and clergy brought some changes to their lives, so that they represent the people well, rather than badly.

There are many who would become priests but they are not willing to take the vow of celibacy, and why should they when they are young and need to have a family. They should change this rule so that it is no longer required of men who would otherwise be priests.

It should be soon that churches commit to those areas of Africa where there is a need for Christianity, but there are those in the church that oppose the expenditure required for this. In future these people must realise that there are people who would learn if we gave them the tools.

However, no-one should train a person to believe in Christ if they need to adopt a different path. If it is to be successful, it must be the heart that decides.

And you should find a way to bring changes in Africa, for many need food and development and yet if we cannot recognise how necessary this is, it may never come.

You must learn that it is crucial that you comply with God's worth and when you do fulfilment will follow. Many beg for food and go hungry, while the rest of the world carries on as though everything is alright. People should no longer beg. They should have a different understanding of good which others could learn. It is necessary now to adjust so that we respect God's rules so that we no longer apply distressing values to our lives but apply God's attitude instead.

You must understand that God's values actually mould the world into a place where the value of a worthwhile life is recognised and that will then create a need to improve it even more.

Start this soon and appreciate its value.

The Writing

That of the need now is to write of the governing attitude that can bring value to our lives. For we are God's people and we bring God's attitude to the people.

And yet I see among us a number of irresolute and upset people who would do God's work but they have lost the need, because they are not happy with the message given.

And that of the Message of God has not carried value of worth since the ones whom He brings to Earth to act for a resolute worth and have held not to their capability, have left the order and adopted irresolute worth instead.

For they have left the church in droves and that need to follow God's character has left them with an abundance of upset instead. For that of forthrightness has been abandoned and instead there has been folly and unreasonable worth held to the work.

Let there be an abandonment of these values that let our friends down so that they may see that God's values mean something and are relevant to modern life.

For there are aspects where the means that man adopts to learn values have been given free expression that cannot value at all the need to live properly.

For it is the wisdom of God's priests and clergy that should bring about change to the character of the people, but that has not happened, and yet they are able to live comfortably and well, and they cannot see that the poor within whom they work at times cannot relate to the value change of God.

For we are all able to call on God to be there when we need, and that need now is for some of those priests and clergy to bring about change in their own lives so that they represent the people well and not badly.

For there are many who would follow the priesthood but they are not able to take that vow of celibacy. And why should they do that when they are able and young and that of the need is to live within the format of a family. Let it be soon that they adjust this rule so that the need no longer requires it of the men who would otherwise be priests.

Let it be soon also that the commitment of churches extends to learning that the forgoing of some of the churches attributes are of worth to a new order of worth in the African areas where there is a need for the governing of people's souls through a Christian belief, but there are those who oppose the expenditure needed. Forthwith let it be that these people learn that there are some who would follow if we gave them tools for learning. But let it be that no one attitude trains someone to believe in Christ if it is their need to be otherwise, for the need must come from the heart if it is to be successful.

And let it be that you formulate a way to bring about change in the Africa region of the world, for there are many who need food and development and yet that may never come if we see not the ready need for it.

Let it be soon that you learn God's compliance with worth must be obeyed and that fulfilment follows, for there is an attitude that all is well about the world and yet there are many people hungry and begging.

Let it be no more that the people beg but bring a different appreciation of good so that it may show others a need to comply also. Let it be soon that you do for the need now is to adjust our lives and give that of worship to God's rules so that a need shows to follow the attitude of God and not follow the value of upset instead.

Let it be soon that you understand that God's values mould the world into a place where the principle of worth is seen, and that vigilant approach shall bring forth a need to generate more worth. Let it be soon that you do this and learn its values.

H

Happiness (Channelled 8 June 2007)

Key Points

- God needs us to be happy.
- We need to find fulfilment.
- Fulfilment powers us on to change.
- If we cannot be bothered to change we cannot be happy.
- Mischief and upset does not help you to progress. It is the sign of a boring life.
- Love brings inner peace and happiness. That is how your future will be if you follow God's values.

A Clear Summary

In this writing, Jesus speaks of us needing to change our lives now to fulfil God's ambition for us to be happy. Without fulfilment we cannot be happy and to progress we must be fulfilled.

He says we are unwilling to change unless we can see a promise of fulfilment and yet if we are happy that will come. Happiness cannot be based on anything other than the soul's fulfilment, and if we resist change we do ourselves no favours.

He needs you to understand that God gives you the basis for a happy life and you have to accept change if you are to reach this level. Everyone has the formula and it is essential to progress and realise the fulfilment that God brings you. The need to be happy leads you along this pathway, unlike the need to cause mischief and upset which only leads you up a blind alley. That is a path taken by people who lead boring lives and have to find their fun in upsetting others.

However, love is God's way and if your pathway is walked with love you will be happy and fulfilled. Those are God's values and they lead to peace within. Stick to them and you will find that love will always endure, because God's Love is all powerful and brings peace and brother/sisterhood within.

The Writing

This is the day that we change our lives to fulfil that ambition of God that we are happy. For we are not happy people if we are not fulfilled and that of the need now is to feel fulfilled in our need to progress. For we are willing not to change if we cannot see fulfilment within our lives, and yet if we can just change that of the ability to be happy, we are able to fulfil all that which is necessary within our lives.

For we are able not to base happiness on anything other than fulfilment to the soul, for we are able not to bring about a happy state by being lethargic in our will to grace that of our need to bring about change.

Let it be you understand now that a grace is given by God to bring you a happy life, and you must bring about the change necessary within your life if you are to attain this. For this is a formula held to all people, that they may feel fulfilled and happy within life and that cannot be lost if we are to bring a need to move on in the fulfilment of God.

Let it be that you understand that there are needs that fulfil our being, and we are led there by the need to be happy. But that cannot be if we adulterate our lives by being of worth to a need for mischief and upset. And yet that can be fun to be mischievous and upset people, if you are leading a boring life. And yes it is so that there are many people who feel it is the way forward; to serve no one and to bring mischief and upset to all those around them, and yet it leads only to a blind alley.

For the way of love is God's way of need. For everyone to learn the way of love is good and shall be excessively worthwhile if it is given the goodness of God's Love to endure within.

Let it be that you learn soon that the pathway of love is given so that you will be happy and fulfilled. And that must be your way forward if you are to give yourself to God's values. For the living of God's values leads to peace within, and it must be adhered to if it is given within the love of God for the establishment of good shall always bring an enduring love within, and that can only be God's values in the making.

For the Will of God is all powerful and shall bring to all who need a way of peace and fraternity within.

Have Faith in God
(Channelled 14 May 2007)

Key Points

- Have faith even when life is not going well.
- Bringing God to a task may produce a solution and to be completely worthwhile this should be followed.
- Generate faith in God and it will change your life.
- We commit ourselves to work sometimes to change our lives.
- God's values must be followed if we are to change for the better.
- We need to follow the guidance given and help ourselves achieve our goal.
- Learn the way to gain full advantage over your future tasks.

A Clear Account

Jesus says that now and then you have to have faith in the future even when it does not look to be working out, because bringing God's value to a task will sometimes formulate an easy way, or it may be difficult, but you must persevere if it is to be completely worthwhile.

Bringing God's values into play may not be rewarding to you unless you follow through completely in understanding and trust.

There is a need now to generate faith in God and it will change your life in an amazing way. You will feel worthwhile and when that happens, it will help you to progress. You will feel the benefit of following that advice.

Sometimes we commit ourselves to projects so that they bring life changes, in which case we must obviously choose what is right so that it is advantageous to us, however you must understand that God's values are to be followed if changes are to be beneficial. That puts us in control, for when we follow guidance we are given, we acquire the values that help us achieve our goal.

You must now learn how to put together a future that is of complete benefit to your tasks.

The Writing

It is necessary now and then to have faith in the way forward even though it does not appear to formulate well, for the giving of God's worth to a task will bring about changes that may formulate an easy approach or a difficult one, and that which is given must be followed if it is to be fully of value.

For a need to serve God's values may not offer an option worthwhile to you if it is not followed in a full and pure level of understanding and trust. For a need now holds to generate faith in God, and this will bring you changes in your life that will follow an amazing pattern. And that will give you faith in your worth being seen, and it will formulate such progression that will make obvious the need to follow the advice.

Let it be that you know now that we give ourselves to such projects necessary sometimes to bring about changes in our lives. And that must obviate the choice we are given that we may choose appropriately and not without an obvious advantage.

Let it be that you understand that God's values are to be followed if we are to bring about change to good. And that must bring mastery to our goal, for our function is to follow the advice given and generate a necessary worth to be advantageous to our goal.

Let it be you learn soon how to formulate a way forth that is of full advantage to the tasks you hold ahead.

Help Others (Channelled 6 June 2007)

Key Points

- Greed shows when one man cannot give to another.
- The overwhelming principle in life is to help change others' lives for the better when your own life improves.
- Find a way to serve others as well as yourself. Your life will be more rewarding.
- You cannot grow fully if you are not as worthwhile to others as you are to yourself.
- To serve God, you must give part of the love you are given.
- Change comes about when a worthwhile way is given goodness.
- Realise this and be worthwhile towards your fellow man.

A Clear Account

In this writing, Jesus explains how man interferes with the progress of others.

It shows greed when one person cannot give to another, for the overwhelming principle in life is to help change others' lives so that they benefit when yours improves.

You need to formulate a way to serve other people as well as yourself, for in that way your life will be fuller, more interesting and worthwhile.

There must be happiness and not upset, and that which you give must produce this, for you yourself will not see growth if you do not include others in your plans.

You are made of love, and to serve God, part of this must be given to others. And that can only be good if you formulate a way that is worthwhile. Understand this, and be worthwhile to your fellow man.

The Writing

It is good to talk now of the interference that mankind makes in his neighbour's need to move forward, for it is an indication of greed when one man cannot give to another, for the overwhelming principle in life is to bring about changes in the lives of all people, so that they may benefit as well as you, when you gain in worth.

Let it be that you formulate a way in your life that you can serve others as well as yourself for your life will be fuller, more interesting and worthwhile if you do so.

For the formulation must bring happiness and not upset, and that given must bring about change and wisdom held to bring about happiness within life, for that of abundant growth cannot be seen if you give not of worth to your neighbour and friend as you would give yourself.

For you are of love made, and a fragment of that must be given towards those around you to serve God. And that must abound in good if you formulate a way that resonates with the good of worthwhile procedure that brings about change.

Let it be soon you realise this and are capable and worthwhile towards to your fellow man.

Help the Poor
(Channelled 12 June 2007)

Key Points

- Some cannot advance in life because they are poor
- They are made poor because of the ones who will not share their wealth.
- Governments, councils and the Church are meant to help those in need but they fail to do so.
- Some generate good but others do nothing.
- There is an obligation to the young, the old and all who suffer.
- The poor also suffer through politics where people defy the need to help and drain all quality from their lives.
- Let it be soon that the Church brands guilty governments as hypocrites.
- Churches must soon find a formula to help the poor rather than to help themselves become richer.

- Let all men stand together in love and face a future according to God's principles.

A Clear Account

Jesus says in this writing that some are unable to progress in life because they are poor. It is not that they have a particular right to be poor, but that it is a result of those who will not share their wealth. And those who fall into that category are governments, councils and above all the Church, who are meant to help those in need but instead bring anarchy of faith by not doing so.

Man cannot be inert, he must generate good. There are some people, who do good things and are faithful for the future, but there are those who do nothing and they must accept blame for those who suffer and are upset by their dismal future.

All mankind must work to bring good and they must feel an obligation to the young, the old and all those who suffer.

The poverty stricken must no longer be without hope and have their futures upset by the defiant rich. They already suffer deranged lives, they do not need the cruelty that is dealt by politics, where their hopes are dashed and every bit of quality is drained from their lives.

Soon we must hear the churches brand such governments as hypocrites and soon the churches themselves must bring about changes so that they help those who are in need, and not just swell their bank balances.

Soon all people must stand together in love and bring about a future according to God's principles.

The Writing

This is to tell of the inert measure of some people's capability; that they are unable to proceed in life because they fall within the category of poor.

Let it be that you understand now that these people have no right given to be poor, but they are made poor by the inert thinking of those who will not share their wealth. And that category applies to governments, councils and above all the Church, who are meant to help the ones of need but hold instead to a need to defy the rules and bring about an anarchy of faith instead.

Let it be that the mentality of man cannot lead to inertness but must lead to a need to generate good. For there are some who will do good, and will be of faith to the future needs. But there are those who will do nothing and they must be blamed for all the ones who suffer and are aggravated by their dismal future.

Let it be that all mankind shall see a way to formulate goodness in this sphere, and be of obligation to the young and old and all who suffer to be about them and for them in all ways.

Let it be no longer that the poverty-stricken shall have no hope and that the rich merely formulate a way of upset for them by defying the need to help. Let it be enough that they suffer deranged lives than they are to be the object of cruelty also. For they are given hope not in the knowing of mankind's need to help, but in a formulation of worth held to political approach. So there are those who hope and are deprived of any zest from the wish given, by the defiance of those following a political need to defy and exhume every scrap of quality left in lives.

Let it be soon that we see the churches brand such governments as hypocrites, and let it be soon that they themselves bring forth the change necessary that shall malleate a formula of worth for all who need, and not for themselves in the need for coffers earned. Let it be soon that all men shall stand together in love and formulate a way that is of sound worth to God's Principles.

I

Institute Of Marriage Part One
(Channelled 16 May 2007)

Key Points

- Within the boundaries of God's laws it is necessary to bring about change, adapting and reformatting where it is not properly set out.
- We are right about the need to generate love between two people, whether it is between a man and a woman, two men, or two women.
- All these are love and must hold the same principles in the act of love.
- The loving of one person is paramount.
- We must be worthwhile and loving towards each other during our time together.
- God's values do not include a need to remain faithful forever. That is a man-made scripture.
- Where there is violence between partners it must end.
- God's power must be understood by everyone. Violence cannot continue if marriage is to be fulfilled according to Christ's needs.
- We may feel we need to retaliate. That is no good. The need is for love and friendship.

- You may be kind and forgiving. If not try and adapt so you can fulfil your contract to each other.
- If you are lesbian you may need to leave a male partner and be with a woman. God permits this as long as the same values are held as between a man and a woman.
- Men and women make changes to accommodate children. A lesbian relationship may not fulfil this so you can compensate by fostering or loving other children.
- A man serves his wife. He cannot be completely fulfilled if partnered by a man when he needs children. It could be difficult to foster.
- The need to serve God by having children when in a male partnership may have to wait.
- A man may leave a man marriage to have a child or he may have a child in a later life.
- Some couples love each other but are concerned about the need to marry. God accepts them.
- It is allowed if two people love each other and set up home together.
- They may formalise marriage, or not yet feel able to fulfil the vows.

A Clear Account

Jesus says here that it is necessary within the scope of God's Laws to bring changes. That must be if we are to adapt and reformat where it is not properly set out.

We are right about the need to generate love between two people and that applies if it is a man and a woman, a man and another man, or a woman and another woman.

All these are love and they are to hold the same principles as that which is defined as the act of love, for the loving of one person is to be of paramount importance in life, and so that this can happen it is allowed that there are two who deem their love to be so important, that they stay together resolutely in love for as long as is needed.

We are fractious by nature and so some may need to move on when others do not. We must be worthwhile to each other during our time together. Some remain together faithfully with one partner, but some need a different dimension in their lives and leave.

If people are to stay together they must love each other and that will then make them faithful. It will also form a basis for a family and all that that brings. However, God's values do not include a need to remain faithful forever, and that is a man made scripture.

But the law only allows that it shall change if the efforts to be loving and wise in a marriage are unsuccessful and there is disdain rather than God's path of love. Hopefully you are wise and able to be loving and worthwhile in your life.

There are some violent people who only find fulfilment through hurting and behaving badly towards their lover. That must not continue and if they are to fulfil marriage according to Christ's needs, there must be an end to the violence. For God's Power must be understood by everyone.

Later on we may find someone who brings out the demon in us and encourage us to retaliate. That is no good. Mankind's fulfilment comes through love and friendship.

You may be in a situation where you wish to improve your marriage and that may be through committing solely to the partnership. Maybe you are a kind and generous person in all ways who is also forgiving but if you are not, try to change as a couple and work together so that you can fulfil your contract to each other.

If you are a lesbian you may not be able to give your love to a man. You may decide to leave him and be with another woman. God permits this as long as you put the same values on the new relationship as if it were between a man and a woman.

For men and women make changes in their lives to accommodate children, whereas you must follow the guideline that there are some parts of life that cannot be fulfilled if there are not two discriminating parents to fulfil the act.

But there are needs and they can be fulfilled by fostering and by loving other children. You should do this.

A man's task however is to serve his wife and if he is partnered by a man he is not fulfilled by being alone. He carries a need to have children. He will not be fulfilled without this love. He may feel cheated if he has no children and may want to foster as compensation, but that can be difficult.

To serve God fully he must wait. He will feel worthwhile as his life improves and he values his partner's needs more, changing God's life process as he does this. He must not try to dictate the situation but accept willingly that that which is brought about by some can cause distress, and that cannot be.

So instead you may choose to leave a male marriage to have a child or have a child in a later life when the formula for your life will be different.

There are also those couples who love each other but are concerned about having to marry. We accept them. All God's manifest power is brought to life and we let it happen as it is willing to happen.

There may be a situation where one person is fulfilled by another and that may be prohibited by law, however it is valued fully where the need is to bring love and set up home together. And if their wish is to love fully and willingly alongside each other and to adapt accordingly, then let it be.

They will formalise a marriage if they wish to be correct, but if they are loving and happy together they may need the freedom. They may not yet feel able to take God's vows and promise to fulfil them.

The Writing

It is a need within God's Laws to bring about change, and that must be necessary if we are to adapt our lives and change that which is not formatted properly and correctly.

Let it be that we are correct about the need to generate love between two people. And that may be between a man and a woman, or a man and a man, or woman to woman. Let it be that all these values are love and they are to be principled as that act of love is defined.

For the loving of one person shall be of paramount importance in a life, and so that may happen, it is given that there are two who will evaluate their love in such a way that it demands that they stay together in love and resoluteness for a time needed.

Let it be that we are fractious by character, and that need to move on may be given more of a need by some but not others.

Let it be that we are worthwhile during our stay together. For the need is now that some remain in the need to stay together so they may remain faithful to their partner, and some may not stay, but will bring a new dimension to their lives by leaving and moving on.

For the need to stay together to fully work, there must be love, and that will bring faithfulness to the many who need it. But that is not all, for it will format a way forward where both people may allow for the generating of a family and all that that brings

Let it be that you know now that God's values do not incorporate a need to remain faithful forever, and that is a man made scripture. But the law allows only that it shall change if the efforts to be wise and fruitful and loving in the marriage bring disdain, and are not allowed to communicate the wisdom of God's pathway through love.

Let it be that you are wise and able to communicate through love, and be able to bring about those changes in your life that are loving and worthwhile.

And there are those who bring masochism to their need, and they think they are fulfilled only when they are hurt or of unreal worth to their lover.

That may not continue, and if the following of Christ's need to fulfil marriage is given, it must be that the assault is finished and got rid of. For it must be that the knowing of God's Power is understood by all and not left by some to interpret.

Let it be that later in life we give ourselves to someone who is of worth to our demonic values and that they bring us a need to retaliate, and that is not good, for the fulfilment of mankind's needs must be to bring love and friendship to any fulfilment.

Let it be also that you feel a need to generate more worth in your marriage. And that may be by evaluating a need to hold to the marriage and not give yourself a need to formulate a worth elsewhere.

Let it be that you are generous and kind and forgiving in all thoughts and actions. But if not, let it be that you try fully to re-enact with each other and bring about changes necessary to fulfil the marriage contract.

Let it be that you are given to be of lesbian approach, and that may damage fully your need to follow other wisdoms and give your love to a man. Let it be that after discourse with your partner you have arrived at a decision to leave him and be with one of the same sex as you. It is permitted by God to do this as long as you evaluate your relationship in the same way as a man and woman would, for they will bring about changes in their lives to accommodate children, and you must follow the guideline that there are some parts of life that cannot be fulfilled if there are not two discriminating parents to fulfil the act.

But there are needs, and these can be fulfilled by fostering and loving other children too. Let it be that you do this.

However a man's task is to be of service to his wife. And if that happens to be that he is partnered by a man, it will fulfil him not to be alone, and that must bring about the need to be fertile and encounter not the upset of a childless life, for that will not fulfil him if he has never known love.

Let it be that you know now that he may demand recompense for not having children and that may bring a need for him to foster also, but that may prove difficult, as he is a man. And that need to serve God fully must wait, and he will feel value as he sees himself improve and love more as a result of changing God's process and bringing about an evaluation of worth towards others' needs.

Let it be that he is seen not to demonstrate wilfulness, but a need to accept willingly that that instigated by some may bring upset if they are to feel fulfilled and that cannot be. So it may be that you choose to leave the fulfilment of a man marriage and have a child, or leave the need to have a child until another life when it would be formulated differently.

Let it be that we accept the ones who need to generate love but are upset about the need to marry. Let it be that we bring all God's Manifest Power to life and let it happen as it is willing to occur, for the fulfilment of one person to another may prohibit a change in the law if there is a degree of good to be seen. But it may evaluate fully in the need to generate love if the willingness to two people is to set up home together.

And if their attitude is to live in full and willing capacity to bring about change and worth to their lives, then let it be. For they will formalise a marriage if they are to be correct and hold an attitude where they are loving and happy together, but they may wish only to be free. And that must evaluate the process as that taken by those not yet able to take the vows of God and bring them a promise of fulfilment.

Institute Of Marriage Part Two
(Channelled 18 May 2007)

Key Points

- It is good if you are sure of your partner's faith-fulness and goodness towards you.
- This does not always apply, particularly where there is violence.
- Those who are unhappy and unable to use love to heal the problems in their marriage must look for change.
- An attempt at reconciliation is the first step if appropriate.
- God's Principles allow that love cannot always heal situations.
- Creating love is paramount, but anger and hate can prohibit this.
- God's Principles still apply when people need to escape anger and find good.
- God's children are allowed to get things wrong.

- Everyone is entitled to change if there is no love.
- Goodness and confidence must be created by those who give and receive love in marriage.
- Be strong and try to bring love into the equation. This love will help bring changes if necessary.
- It is miserable if there is no love or visible good in a partnership.

A Clear Account

It is good if you are assured that your partner is faithful and worthwhile to you, but this does not apply to everyone, and certainly not where there is violence.

They need to change in whatever way is necessary, because there cannot be a future if there is no return of love and only hate, anger or distress.

All those who are unhappy and unable to heal their marriages through love, must look towards changes. It cannot make everything right if that is what you want so you must first try to bring about reconciliation if it is appropriate.

God's principles accept that where there is a lot of distress and bad feeling, love cannot always heal a situation.

God needs to help when His principles are being followed, by salvaging good but it can require a change of direction. For there is a need to create love and this is paramount, but it is impossible to do so in a situation of great anger and hate. There is a true need for change if it will improve a situation.

You must understand that God's Principles apply when people need a release from anger, and to find something good within their lives. For they are God's children and they must be given the right to get things wrong, and also to escape a situation if they cannot reconcile it. All people deserve change in their lives if there is no love.

Love must be brought to the fore through what is given. Everyone is entitled to benefit from God's love, and if it is not possible to have a happy and content marriage, there can be no justification in denying love.

Marriage cannot be an affront to all those who suffer through the partnership. It must be a place of conciliation for those who give and receive the love they need and they must create a way that brings goodness and confidence to the fore.

Many are not confident of their partner and they may feel that the marriage will not go well if they are not resolute. This will be borne out if they feel lonely and do not behave in a worthwhile way. For it is necessary to be strong so that they can bring love into the equation, because the change it brings will not be worthwhile to some, and yet it will enable them to move forward in God's gaze and bring about changes.

You must feel that the remedy can serve God and that it will bring the changes needed. Because it is miserable if there is no visible good and love is not there.

But instead, it serves good if there is change without it changing your character.

The Writing

It is good if you know that your partner is good and will be faithful and worthwhile entirely. But this is not true of all people, and it cannot be true where there is violence.

It is for those people to bring about change where it is necessary to do so. For a way forward cannot be found if by generating love you feel no response, and there is hate or pure anger and upset.

For the need now to bring about change applies to all those who are unhappy and unable to rectify their marriages through a loving way. But it cannot rectify everything if that is what you wish, and you have to bring about some changes yourself that attempt at reconciliation first if that is appropriate.

Let it be that you know now that God's principles accept that there are deviations from a rule if there are paramount upsets and unreal emotions felt, and that the giving of love cannot always rectify a situation.

Let it be that you know now that God's willingness to help brings about a change where God's principles can be seen, but the need to obey them has been altered through a need to rectify a situation, and bring about worth.

For the need to generate love is paramount and this cannot be if there is anger and hate in abundance. But the verification for a change can be seen if the need is to generate better behaviour and worth to a situation.

Let it be that you know now that God's principles apply to all those who crave for a period of peace from anger, and need that which is of goodness in their lives.

For they are God's children and they must be given the right of misdemeanour and if necessary a way that is right for their need if they are unable to reconcile the situation.

Let it be that you know now that all people deserve to bring about change in their lives if they are unable to perpetuate love. And that given must bring about love to the fore. For it is given that all people shall benefit from God's love, and that need to justify it cannot be if the way is not clear for a happy contented marriage.

Let it be that you know now that the institute of marriage cannot be an affront to all those who are maligned and upset in their lives. It must be a place of conciliation, where those who love are given that love they need and they must formulate a way that provides goodness and brings confidence to the fore.

For there are many who are not confident of their partner, and they may feel that it does not bode well for their marriage if they are not resolute.

This is right and it will bring right to the equation if they feel loneliness and worthless behaviour too. For it will bring about a change that some will not feel worthwhile. Yet it is so, for it will bring a need to tread forth in the gaze of God and be worthwhile in a need to bring about change.

Let it be that you feel that remedy is to be of service to God and that that will bring about changes necessary.

For it is a dismal approach indeed, if goodness is not seen and love not held? But it is a good service that is held to and not a rearranging of character that will bring about changes.

J

Just How Much Do You Value Life?
(Channelled 22 April 2007)

Key Points

- Are you on a treadmill to nowhere?
- Happiness depends on aspects of your life that fulfil you and not the purchases that have put you in debt.
- Why not create a fulfilment account which can be paid into at any time?
- Create a time of happiness and ecstatic love.
- God's pathway may sometimes seem less attractive.
- God's pathway is the best one to pick.
- It brings abundant growth and does not bankrupt you.
- Discern between the reward of money and fulfilment measured in health and worth.

A Clear Account

Jesus asks here just how much you value your life or whether you are on a treadmill to nowhere. The formula for happiness includes aspects of your life that are really important to you and fulfil you. These do not include the purchases that have left you with payments to make.

Imagine you are fortunate and able to buy all you need, however that is not likely if you only have enough for one payment. Instead, why not create a fulfilment account which can be paid into at any time. This way you will create a time both of happiness and ecstatic love, and that will motivate you to create even more value in your life. For God's pathway can seem rather less attractive at times but it costs less and the growth you achieve is amazing, so it must be the better path to pick.

Imagine that you are celebrating the huge growth from walking God's pathway and it has not bankrupted you as the other path can, and you have still managed some time off with your loved one. You have not spent so long in the office or on the phone with bills paid in a miserable way instead of feeling you have received full value.

If you are to live life fully you neither have to be mean or tough, you can discern between the reward of money or fulfilment which is measured in health and feeling worthwhile.

The Writing

You should consider if your life is really worthwhile or are you on a treadmill to nowhere?

For the formula to happiness is to bring those aspects of your life that are truly important to you, and bring you fulfilment, and not those that are bought with difficulty and make you unhappy with the payments you have to raise.

Let it be that you are fortuitous and able to fund all the things you need, but that is not likely if you are able only to afford the one level of payment and that is poor.

Let it be that you create instead an account of worth and that can be paid into at any time. For you will create a time of happiness and ecstatic love. And it shall bring you a need to serve more fully in generating the worth needed. For God's pathway seems less attractive at times, but it must be the favourable one for it costs less and has abundant growth.

Let it be that you celebrate an abundant growth within the need to serve God's pathway, and are not led to insolvency by the path that dictates that you should not take time off with your loved one, and that that of giving love is to be stopped as there is too much time spent on the phone or in an office; so that bills have to be paid in a miserable fashion and not happy with the rhetoric that that given has been of value.

Let it be that you are neither miserly or robust if you are to give of your life fully and let it be that you learn soon how to discern between that of reward to the value of money, and that of fulfilment measured in good health and worth felt.

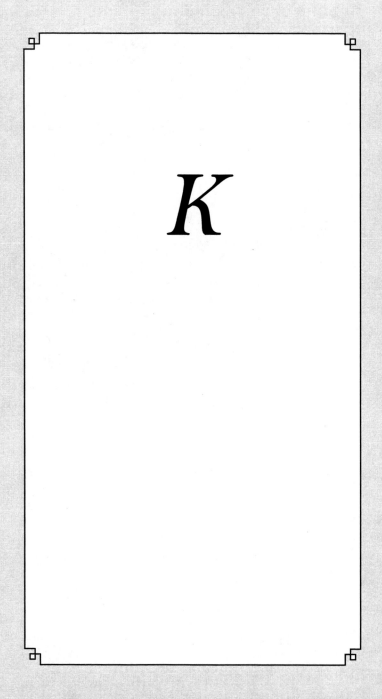

K

Keep Faith with God
(Channelled 26 April 2007)

Key Points

- Life involves changes so we ask God's help but if it is not quickly given we can feel let down and that God does not care.
- God does care and gives where it is needed.
- Alternatives may have to be given but these are always better.
- Sometimes God brings you nothing. This is because your pre-life choices demanded this situation, when you specified particular experiences to learn through your life, so this is your choice and not God's.
- God will not interfere with your choices.
- You must live your choices fully and embrace all parts of them.
- Never doubt God if you lose a loved one. He is there to bear the sorrow with you.
- God replenishes you.

- These facts come from the Lord Jesus Christ who knows the Father's Divine Information as it must be given.

A Clear Account

Jesus says here that we have to accept changes in our lives and at these times we may ask for God's help. He says that if the help does not manifest quickly we can lose faith and think that God does not care, but He does and He will give where it is needed. In fact, if He cannot provide a particular solution He will bring a better one. However there are occasions when He will bring nothing, because when you made your pre-life choices you may have chosen to experience certain situations, and if He brought a solution He would be breaking the contract He made with you, and this is not allowed. It must be as you chose. He gave you life and He gives you everlasting love but He will not take away areas of your learning.

You may feel this is cruel and unjust but it is according to your choice and you must embrace this and live it fully.

You should not doubt God if you lose a loved one or suffer some other great loss, because God is with you, bearing your sorrows and pain with you. He replenishes you when you need it and He eases your mind and conscience when you allow it, but it is not unjust of God that the situation happened. Just like others, you have chosen and you have a contract with God that He will not interfere if the feeling to be experienced is not one you have lived before.

You must understand this. Read this information and believe it for you are being told what I receive, and I am the Lord Jesus Christ so I know the Father's Divine Information as it must be given.

The Writing

It is necessary in our lives to undertake changes and to this end we may feel we need God's help, so we ask for it.

But if it has not manifested fully within the timescale given, we feel let down because we have not what we want; what we justify in our own minds, and it is upsetting. So then we feel that God does not care. But He does care. And He will give where it is needed.

But if it is not there He will bring an alternative of better quality for the need shown. If it is necessary, He will bring nothing, if it is to be a lesson learnt. And He will fulfil whatever you need, whenever you need, but it must be on your original 'Need' list.

For you have specified needs to learn through life, and that must be your choice and not His. For He has given you life and everlasting love, but He will not take you away from a need to live that which is important to your learning.

You may think this is cruel and unjust, but it is as you choose. And as you make this choice it is for you to live it fully and embrace all that it brings.

It may be that you have lost a loved one or have endured a great loss of upsetting worth in your life. Let it not be that you doubt God is there for you. For He is there to bear your sorrows with you and endure the pain with you.

For He will replenish you when you need it, and will bring an easing of mind and conscience, as you allow it to happen.

But there is no dynamic that says that it is unjust of God to let it happen. For you have chosen, as has the other person or people with you. And you have a contract to keep with God, that He will not interfere or take from you, that which is original feeling, and not one you have lived before in a need to serve the way forward.

Let it be you understand, this and give your willing thoughts to consume and believe the facts here. For you are told as I am given. And I am the Lord Jesus Christ so I am of worth to knowing the Father's Divine Information as it must be given.

L

Last Rites (Channelled 24 June 2007)

Key Points

- The last rites are given as a sanctimony that God's path shall not fail following the Catholic way of the Christ.
- Articulate people give the last rites but some forget to include the confession to release the soul completely from sin.
- Some allow the sins of the father to be left.
- Many are confused by this
- Many sins are inherited. To be free of these beyond doubt there must be elimination at birth and at death.
- Many inherit the effects of past failure and that must be eliminated to allow someone to progress fully for the future.

A Clear Account

Jesus says that the Last Rites confound many people. They are given to many who worship God through Jesus.

This is when they serve as God's assurance that his pathway will not fail and provide a need to follow Christ through the Catholic faith.

Only the Catholic Church uses these rites to serve the community. The reason for them is to bring about change for the spirit so that it can be released from the body and ascend to heaven's door.

There are articulate priests who give the Rites well, following procedure, but others forget to bring about confession to release the soul from sin. They think the need is to forgive fully the person's sins but they allow the sins of the father to remain.

Many are confused by this for many reasons. However, many sins are inherited and to be free of those beyond doubt they must be eliminated at birth and at death. Many are affected by failure in the past and this must be cleared from their lives so that they can be fully worthwhile to the future.

The Writing

There is a need to write lastly about a subject that confounds many people and that is the Last Rites.

It is true that these are given to many who are honoured to follow the pathway of God through Jesus; and the need for the Last Rites is given as a sanctimony that God's pathway shall not fail and shall bring about a need to follow the Catholic way of the Christ.

Let it be that you understand now that only those of Catholicism use the rites for serving the community, but their need is to bring about change for the spirit so that it may be released from the elaborate cage of the body, and be allowed to soar to the heights needed that it may reach an angelic door to the heavenly host.

Let it be that there are articulate people who give the Last Rites well and follow procedure, but there are others that forget to bring about confession so that the soul may be released from sin. For they are not elaborate in their thinking but they think that the need is to forgive fully and abundantly in sin, but to allow the sins of the father to be left.

For there are many who are confused about this and there are many reasons. Let it be that you understand now that there are many sins inherited and to be free of these beyond doubt there must be an elimination both at birth and at death. For there are many who inherit worth held to past failure and that must be eliminated from their lives so that they can be of worth fully to the future.

(I asked some questions on this subject and received the following answers;

Q. Is there an equivalent (of the Last Rites) for other Christian religions?

A. Yes there is but it only countenances part of the way of Catholicism, so it does not entail forgiveness to the same extent.

Q. Does that mean that other religions carry sins further in their lives?
A. Yes it does in some cases but not all as it is considered not to be a faith issue in all countries.

Q. Does that mean that people of other religions still carry the sins of their fathers through their eternal lives?
A. Yes. It is in accordance with God's rules that no man can be exemplified fully until he is absolved of all sin, and so some do actually carry the sins of some who have lived before. And they must be absolved of all sin if they are to service fully the needs of life before them. Let it be that you understand now that God's purpose is to simplify the mystery and not complicate it. Let it be that you adjust your lives accordingly and be of worth by praying for absolution of all crimes held unto you and all sins held unto you, both past and present. Let that be of need unto future needs for the quality of God to be seen and carried forward.)

Listen to the Advice you are Given
(Channelled 14 May 2007)

Key Points

- You receive a great deal of advice in your life. Some of it is useful and some is not.
- Advisors may advise according to their own needs instead of aiding your progress.
- We may formulate advice that is ridiculous and negative. That is not good. Our thought process has been wrong.
- It is necessary to consult God. His advice will be worthwhile.
- Be alone in your thoughts, concentrate on the subject and have faith. God will send the formula needed to help yourself and others.
- There is no safety issue as warned in the writing called Meditation, because your communication with God is spontaneous and not prolonged.

A Clear Account

You receive many levels of advice during your life. Some is useful, some is not. It can depend on whether the advice given has been formulated according to the advisor's needs, or with a view to helping you progress.

Not all advice is good, and it may not fit your needs.

It takes care to provide advice because we are giving someone else a need to progress in apparent love and care according to their needs, but we may not formulate a wise and positive solution. Maybe that person needs other ideas rather than ours, so that is no good, we would be wrong to advise in this situation and we may impede them rather than help them. So it is necessary to follow God's thinking which will be appropriate to the task. Use this and you will find it worthwhile.

First ensure you are able to be on your own with your thoughts. Concentrate on the one thing and think only of this, for you are about to communicate on a level where you will work out tasks that are worthy to God's name, so have faith in that which is given.

Meditate with God so that the formula you need is sent and that will bring trust and worth to the process.

Use this for your own problems to help others, so you obtain a solution through God's process.

Footnote; in the writing of Meditation, emphasis is put on the safety aspect of doing so on your own, and that it should only be carried out by someone very experienced when used to directly contact spirit. In the case referred to here the contact through meditation is spontaneous rather than prolonged so there is no problem.

The Writing

You are given many levels of advice in your life and some of it is useful and some isn't.

For it to be of best use you must consult your advisors and see whether it is advice given because they have formatted a way according to their own needs, or whether it is about giving you the need to move on.

For not all advice is of good worth and proportion to the task, and it may not fit the needs you hold.

Formulating advice must be a careful act, for we are giving someone else a need to move on in a way that is of apparent love and care to their need. But we may formulate that which is of absurd use and negative thinking. For it may be that the person of whom we care to help, is needing other decisions and other formulations than the one we have in mind. And that will not do. For we are about to give our advice and the deliberation, and our thought process has been wrong. It is a wrong calculation and may impede their way forward instead of help.

So it is necessary to bring the formula necessary to the work and that can be done in a way that holds to God's thinking and shall be worthwhile to the task.

Let it be that you use it for the need shows to be worthy of it.

You will first attend to a need to bring about the changes necessary, so that you are alone in thought. Let it be that you give up your thinking to one task, and let it be that you generate a full thought process to it. For you are about to communicate on a level where you will formulate tasks worthy to be of God's knowing, and that shall bring you a need to generate faith in the subject given.

Let it be that you formulate through meditating with God so that He can send you the formula necessary. And that will bring great faith and worth to the process.

Let it be that you use this process and it will bring you a formula necessary to the helping of others.

Let it be that you also use this when you need a problem solving so you are able to provide a solution through God's process and no other.

Let it be soon that you learn this

Footnote; it is necessary not to attach the same importance level of meditation as that in the writing of Meditation, for although that can be reached as a solitary person that is of worth to the realms of spirit, it cannot defy the need for safety as it will be spontaneous rather than prolonged.

Live a Good Life
(Channelled 21 June 2007)

Key Points

- Many are at risk by leading a life of sin.
- It is necessary to cut down sin and restore good.
- The future is not of value when we steal, rape or commit other crimes.
- There is a need to live in a good way.
- Goodness brings justice and worth to our lives.
- It is better to be worthwhile than not.

A Clear Account

There is a need to cut down the effect of sin in the world and restore good.

The future cannot be of value when we steal, dispose of stolen items, rape or commit many other crimes.

It is necessary to extend goodness. Goodness brings us all to a point where we can account for our lives in a worthwhile and just way. You must realise soon that it is more valuable to you to be worthwhile than to not be.

The Writing

There is a need now to write about the upsetting risk that befalls many who enter into a life of sin. For they may be of worth to the knowledge that a life given to sin is of worth to God also, but that need now is to bring down the effectiveness of sin and allow goodness to be restored.

For the way ahead cannot be of value if we are stealing, or offloading stolen goods, raping or many other upsetting values in the world. But it can be said that there is a need to extend the life of goodness, for that of goodness brings all things together that are worthwhile, and brings us to a place where we can account for our lives with justice and worth.

Let it be that you soon realise that there is more value in worth held than in that of worth upset.

Love and Money
(Channelled 27 May 2007)

Key Points

- It is necessary to live life to the full and bring God to our work.
- Mankind has to learn new skills and bring love to it.
- Giving God's love is paramount.
- Some kill, fight and hate in the pursuit of love. This is not good.
- Some generate love and create quality in the world.
- Nowadays some give all their love to money instead they should serve their neighbour in a loving way.
- Some endure hardship through distress and deprivation.
- Mankind must move on to love others in life rather than follow his own need for money.

- Although life is nothing without love, it cannot have equality without money.
- Money can help you change others' lives for the better.
- Give your love to a project where it is worthwhile and the benefit is visible. Use money in the right way and bring quality to the many lives you touch.

A Clear Account

Jesus says here that it is necessary to live life fully and bring God to our work, for mankind has to fulfil many things in a lifetime. He has to learn a new skill and bring love to it, for it is of the greatest importance to give God's love, for it must not cause distress. For some loves do bring this and that is not good for anyone.

There are some loves that are destructive. Some kill for others, and there are some who fight or create a feeling of hate in their need to seek out love until they die and this is a poor choice.

On the other hand there are others who generate love in their life and bring great quality to the world. Where there is hate they have to fight for good and where there is lust, love is devalued and that must not be, so some bring changes according to God's need and once again there is love in the world.

Nowadays some would give all their love to money. But in truth the principle brought to man is to serve his neighbour and to do it lovingly. For love endures the hardship of deprivation and distress. And this must change mankind and help him move on purposefully and willingly, giving his love to others and not to money.

For life has no value without love, yet it also needs money, for creating money means that people are able to change others' lives for the better.

So be one of those people. Give your love to a project that brings quality to lives, so that the value can be seen and the benefit is evident. Do it soon. Realise there is power in money if you use it right. Learn that and bring quality and justice to the lives you touch.

The Writing

We need to discuss the need to survive life in the fullest capacity and bring God to our work.

It is true that mankind must fulfil many things in his lifetime, for he must fulfil that which is of option to learning a new skill and fulfilling a need to generate love within that capacity.

For that need now to give of God's love is paramount and it must not bring about upset in the doing.

For some loves do bring about upset and it is not good for anyone to endure. For there are those who will kill to be of service to someone, and there are others who will fight or generate hate in their quest to be loved, for they will never eliminate the need to seek love until they pass from life, and it is not good to be of this obtuse choice.

But there are those who will generate love in their life and they bring a love of great quality to the world. Where there is hate they must battle for good and where there is lust there is a dereliction of love and that cannot be; so there are those who bring about the changes of God's preference so that there is love again in the world.

As you know, there are those nowadays who would give all their love to one thing and that is money. But it is a verification of God's worth, that that given to man is to bring about a different principle and that is to serve his neighbour, and to do it with love.

For that given to love must endure the hardships of deprivation and worthless upset. And it must bring about change to the character of mankind and give him a need to move on purposefully and willingly to give his love to his brothers and sisters in life and not to his own need for finance.

For what is life if it is not met by love? And yet it cannot be of solid quality if it has not money too. For there is a need to generate money and it can bring about qualities to people that can be of willingness to change the lives of other people for the better.

Let it be that you are one of those people. Let it be soon that you give your love and wisdom to a project where that of worth can be felt and the benefit gauged.

Let it be soon that you realise what power there is in money if you use it right. Let it be soon that you learn this and bring right and worth to the many lives that you touch.

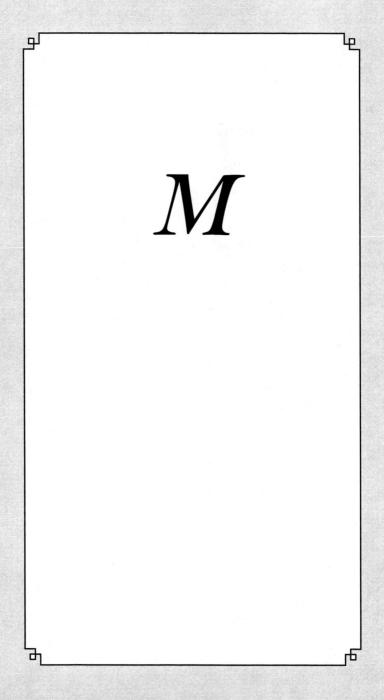

M

Meddlers and Cults
(Channelled 3 June 2007)

Key Points

- Some meddle in others' efforts to be worthwhile to God.
- Some are active, but not towards God. They are apprehensive and fear being pushed into something that is not worthwhile to them.
- People are wrong to hesitate because they need to be alert and ready to fulfil God's needs.
- Meddlers will not leave them alone and try to force them.
- Those who join cults that upset everyone who goes near are only authorities on upset.
- First be worthwhile to God.
- Encourage others to be conversant with the real God.
- There are many ways to serve God and all include His love.

- Adjust your life if necessary and bring the real love of God and not upset to your soul.

A Clear Account

Jesus states here that there are those who meddle when others seek to serve God, but not actively.

These are people who are active, but not towards God. They are uneasy, and fear they may be forced into a way of life that is not appropriate to their need.

They are wrong to be uneasy. They need to be attentive to God's needs and fulfil them. However, some people will not leave them alone. They interfere because they feel that they must overcome their indecision, but that is absurd, for the ones they meddle with will conform as much as they are able.

But where people are attached to a cult or irrational group that evicts all who are not conversant with it, they become authorities on distress and little else because of the rules and trouble they inflict on all who come near.

They must first be meaningful to God and not bring trepidation or fear to those who blunder in an attempt to live in a God-like existence. Instead they need to be familiar with the real God and not worship an idol meant only for bitterness and ill will.

Understand now that there are many ways to serve God, and all of them are given with God's love. Because they are attached to your higher self – your soul – they cannot diminish in their role within your life.

If you need to do so, adjust your life and fill it with God's real love. Forget false and irrational values. These are not worthy of your attention and will only distress your soul if you let them.

The Writing

It is necessary today to talk of the need for relinquishing activity on the meddling front, for there are those who are great meddlers in the activities of those who seek to be of worth to God but not in an active state.

Let it be that they are active people but they are not active towards God, for they are apprehensive about the need to serve God, and they fear they may be catapulted into a way of life that is unreal and of unworthy status to their need.

Let it be that they are incorrect in the need to be apprehensive, because that need is to be awake to the needs of God and to fulfil them, but there are those who will meddle and not leave them alone if they feel that they have to overcome the anxiety about conforming. But that is absurd, for as much as they are capable, they can conform.

But if a need shows to be attached to a cult or an irrational group that evicts all those who are not conversant with their cult, they are authorities only with the upset and unreal measure of their rules and upset all those who come near.

But they must be of real worth to God first and not bring apprehension and upset to all those who blunder with attempts to be of God like existence, but bring unto them a need to be conversant with the real God, and not an adulation of an idol meant only for acrimony and upset.

Let it be that you learn now that there are many ways to serve God and all of them are given with the love of God, for they are all attached to the higher self that is your soul, and they cannot be diminished in role within your life.

Let it be you soon learn the need to adjust your life if you need, and bring it to the love of God in real terms and not those of upset and unreal worth, for they are not worthy of your attention but of upset to your soul if you let it happen.

Meditation (Channelled 28 April 2007)

Key Points

- Meditation is a calming part of the day if you make space for it.
- It can release stress and promote wellbeing.
- To do it fully you need to be with a professional.
- Alone you can reach partial calm and wellbeing.
- Use sounds like the sea, a ticking clock or certain music to relax.
- Intensity of thought power comes with a sitting with a medium, bringing information and restoration.
- Partial restoration when you are alone is helpful too. It brings contentment to the mind and soul.
- Sitting within a circle with a medium is for meditation that changes attitudes.
- Information comes from a higher source.

- There is a need for safety so one person does not communicate alone with spirit realms unless they are very experienced.

A Clear Account

Meditation can be a real calming point in your day if you make the time for it.

It can release you from stress and promote a feeling of wellbeing. But you must first practice it with a professional to do a full meditation, otherwise do a partial meditation on your own and you will achieve calm and wellbeing to a lesser level.

An aid to relaxing can be sounds like the sea, the ticking of a clock or certain types of music.

To reach full meditation it has to be that you connect with the spirit realms and sit with others using a medium. This brings an intensity of thought to the medium, vast information and fully restores you.

But you can feel restored sitting on your own doing a partial meditation. The release will bring contentment both to mind and soul.

Full meditation is for those who sit in a circle and receive information from a higher source. For safety reasons you should not sit alone for this unless you are very experienced.

The Writing

This is such a calming point in your day if you make space for it. It can release you from all the stress you carry if you allow it and it can promote a feeling of wellbeing.

But you have to practice it, and that can only be done by a professional being with you to do it fully unless you partially calm and restore wellbeing by being in repose with a calming sound like the sea or the ticking of a clock or the generating of worth held by listening to some music.

For the restoring of worth can be done in two ways, but it must manifest itself fully only through the way of attaching oneself to the spiritual realms and being worthwhile to a several minute sitting within the power of one mind upon several.

For there are several who are within the power at that one time and that must bring intensity of thought for the one transposed to act as medium to all. And that can bring a volume of information and restoration felt.

But if you bring only a partial restoration felt due to being on your own, it will also bring a restoration of worth within your mind and a contentment held to be of service to God's values held, for it will bring a release that can content and restore with an aim to satisfy a need to generate worth. If that is felt, all is well and it is able then to content the mind, for the wherewithal is to bring contentment to the soul and not an attitude change, which is brought only by a need to sit within a circle and receive information from a higher source.

Let it be that you understand there is a need for safety and therefore it cannot be managed that one person may sit alone to receive information unless they are very experienced

N

Need for Peace
(Channelled 27 May 2007)

Key Points

- Mankind's character must change to bring about more peace and value to life, rather than war and conflict.
- There are too many enemies in the world and too few peacemakers.
- There is a tendency to declare hostilities if agreements are not reached.
- There is a need for peace rather than war and following this would cultivate love between nations.
- We must refocus our minds and stop upsetting others because they are poorer or live in a different way.
- What is good for one is not always good for all.

- There is a need not to hate terrorists. They are misled into feeling and cultivating hate and distress.

- Some bring about upsetting situations in the name of Allah. They are not trained to be worthwhile to Allah they are trained to be worthwhile to an army commander, who cultivates hate, for he has no conscience or value.

- The problem can be met by love if everyone is worthwhile to all Muslims. Giving love has great value.

- Through loving all people we achieve power because lust and hate cannot last if love and value dominates negotiations.

A Clear Account

Jesus says that mankind's character must change so there is less war and conflict and more peace and value to life, but first the attitude must be meaningful. You cannot upset people if you then want them to be friends.

With so many enemies in the world there are not enough peace makers to create warmth and tolerance among them, because the emphasis is on war, not on peace. There is a tendency to send in the troops and declare hostilities if people do not agree with the policies of others. They declare war in what they mistakenly feel is a just cause, but maybe the feeling is not so within them.

For they are forthright in their own views, and will destroy the belief of others, and bring nothing but grief and trouble to all.

There is a strong need now for peace, not war and conflict and it must be followed because it will cultivate love between nations. Where there was once conflict, it can promote a need for fellowship and value, and where this continues, happiness and good can only follow.

For those who are forthright in the cause of peace can create it in a loving and kind way, and that will leave people a need to be constructive towards good rather than harm.

We must refocus our minds on the need for peace, and lose the need for displeasing other people or countries because they are poorer or different to us. We must leave them to be true to their own needs, so that they can enjoy a life of good in their own way, and not evil.

There are many faces of good and you must understand this. What is good for one is not always good for all.

However there is no need to generate hate for terrorists. You must understand that they are misled into feeling and generating hate and distress in the world in the name of their cause.

There are those people who create trouble and distress in the name of Allah. But they are not trained to be worthwhile to Allah, they are trained to be obedient to an army commander, and he is the one who has cultivated hate, and it is he who will change the world through crime and distress if he can. He is not a person with a conscience or any value.

But the problem can be met by love if everyone is honest and true to all people of the Muslim faith, for it can bring about change in a great way.

The giving of love and understanding has great value. It is very powerful and the way to progress is to love our neighbour, and not hate them. We must not bring rage or prejudice to the table of peace, neither must we obstruct peace, but we must gain in wisdom and love. For it is through loving all people that we achieve power and not through lust, hate and other offensive ways. There is strength in these ways, but they cannot last if love and value dominates negotiations and exchanges.

The Writing

Let it be that we talk about the need for mankind to change his character so that there is less war and aggravation and more peace and worth.

But if there is to be peace there has first to be an attitude that is worthwhile. For the need for peace cannot generate upset among men if they are to be friends and not enemies. But there are so many enemies in the world that there are not the peacemakers to create a warmth and tolerance amongst them.

For the need now is to create war and abide not in peace, but deliver a warship or upset a country in a declaration of hostilities threatened, if they are averse to moving in the way needed by some. For they are the declarers of war where they advance fully in a need to salvage something of good but not feel the good within them.

For they are forthright agitators and they will upset the cause where it is possible and it will bring grief and upset to all involved. For there is a need now to bring about peace and not war, and it cannot be that this is not followed. For it will bring about a generation of love between all nations. And it will give to some a need for fellowship and worth where before there was conflict. And if this need is followed through, it can only bring happiness if the goodness is seen.

For the forthrightness of some shall be seen to be of overt worth to peace if it is generated in love and kindness. And that need to shell and to bomb will leave those with intent to harm in a sacrilegious way of up-set no more, if they are defined to be of worth instead to good.

Let it be soon that we adjust our minds to peace and not war, and release that need to deprecate and upset other colonies and countries afar, who do not live as we do, but employ that way which is of worth to poverty not but a symbolism of wealth; that they may be worthwhile in a way intended to man and can be given that of worth and left in peace to enjoy a life of good and not evil.

Let it be soon that you realise that there are many facets to good, and that that which is good for one can-not always be good for all.

But that of the need now is not to generate hate where terrorists are involved, but to understand that they are misled, and that upset to the character has brought about a need to generate hate and upset in the world.

For there are those who will bring upset if it is in the name of Allah, but they are not trained to be of worth to Allah, but only to a battalion master, and it is he who has brought about the need for hate and it is he who will change the world by crime if he can, and not an individual who has conscience and worth.

But it can be met by love shown to all people who are of the Muslim faith, and that can bring about change in a great way. For the giving of love is of powerful worth and that shall be the way forward if we are given to love our neighbours and not hate them. And to bring not obstruction and rage to the Table of Peace, but a gaining of love and wisdom instead.

For it is the loving of all people that brings about power, and not lust and hate and all things offensive.

For there is a might seen in all these things but they cannot last if there is a love and worth given to all negotiations and worths exchanged.

Nuclear Power
(Channelled 21 June 2007)

Key Points

- There is a prime need to eradicate nuclear fuel from the world.
- It is lethal in warfare and generating power.
- There is a lack or moral judgement in making nuclear fuel.
- An alternative must be found soon.
- It brings a terrible power to the world threatening everyone's security.
- There is a need to refocus on generosity of spirit rather than recklessness.
- The outcome of a nuclear war is doubtful and thinking of it as a source of power is abysmal.
- Coal fired stations bring less terror than a nuclear power station.
- Stop destroying areas of land in the need to provide Palm Oil. Use water.

- Condemn the production of nuclear bombs in the 21st century.
- Such systems upset the world.

A Clear Account

Many issues are not good in the world, but the greatest need is to eradicate nuclear fuel. It is lethal in warfare and in generating power.

But it is not heartless behaviour that brings about its manufacture, it is a lack of morals. The future cannot be truly worthwhile until an alternative is found.

There are many alternatives ready to be used and it will be a happy day when policy makers bring about change, for nuclear fuel will not bring happiness, but a terrible power that threatens everyone's security.

You must refocus your thoughts on a need to show generosity of spirit and not recklessness.

Find an alternative soon for the outcome of a nuclear war is doubtful, and as an idea for power it is abysmal. Coal fired stations would bring less horror for the future than nuclear power stations.

Do not destroy areas of land for the production of Palm Oil. Use water and condemn the need to develop nuclear bombs in the 21st century.

It is systems like these that cause upset throughout the world. You must change this soon.

The Writing

There is an issue to bring about the radiation that is experienced around the world.

There are many issues that are of goodness not unto the world, and that one of prime need is to eradicate the world of nuclear fuel. For it is lethal in all forms of warfare and generating power.

But it is made not with abandonment of heart to the world's needs but an abandonment of moral worth. For the way forth cannot continue in true worth until there is found an alternative scheme to that of nuclear power.

For there are many alternatives ready to be used in its stead, and it shall be a happy day when the ones who dictate policy bring about change, for it will format not happiness, but a terrible power within the world that threatens the security of everyone.

Let it be that you adjust your thoughts to a need to demonstrate that worth that gives for generosity of spirit and not recklessness. Let it be that you find an alternative soon for there are many reasons to doubt the outcome of a war that is of nuclear proportion, and that of the need to use it in power stations is abysmal thinking.

Let it be that you adjust your thoughts so that a value can be put upon serving the community with coal fired stations again as they were of service to the community, and yet they bring less horror to the way forth than a nuclear power station.

Let it be that you adjust your thoughts to a need to burn those areas of land not that are flagrantly destroyed in a need to provide Palm Oil, but bring also a need to adjust to involving a way forth held to water.

Let it be that you bring about condemnation of the acts made to bring about a nuclear bomb in the 21st century, for it is systems such as these that cause upset throughout the world.

Let it be soon you change this.

O

Others' Lives (Channelled 18 May 2007)

Key Points

- Many choose to live a life according to others' wishes.
- Some choose to dictate others' lives.
- Each person should follow God's rules only, because there are individual needs that apply to each one.
- Some are affected by others' ambitions for them, but this does not fulfil their own needs.
- To realise a full and worthwhile life, live that which is formulated to suit you.
- A person may need to learn through an upsetting situation if they are to progress.
- We are here to learn goodness and worth for our souls. To accomplish that, hardship may be a necessary lesson.
- Evaluate, aim only that which is challenging, not just an indication of ability.

A Clear Account

Jesus reminds us here that certain rules are necessary in life and this is the time where some choose to live life according to others' needs, similarly when some dictate others' pathways.

There are many things in life and it's good for people to experience those necessary to each. In that way they live only by God's rules.

But some are ambitious for others and leave them with no opportunity to justify their own needs. God cannot live your life, and you live that which you choose if you are to live a full and worthwhile life.

Giving love must not impede your judgement where a person may learn from a potentially upsetting situation, but we cannot remove them from the hardship. They have to learn so they can progress.

Be resolute in creating happiness. It will not be worthwhile unless it is a correct choice. First evaluate the situation, and then if it is worthwhile to all parties you can restore what is needed. But if difficulty is necessary as a learning stage, it must be allowed to continue and this loving act will help its success.

For we are here to learn what is good and worthwhile to our souls and if this includes hardship then it is good to be able to accomplish that. If there is a way out of a situation and it is not right for us it will not be good.

So evaluate and help towards the challenges of life and not just appreciating the abilities to be reached in life.

Learn the difference.

The Writing

It is necessary in life to observe certain rules and that is true of this next worth. For a need holds to many who choose to live a life according to the wishes of others and they are not right for thinking this. Nor is the person right who will insist that another person lives according to their reason.

For many things abound in life and it is good to experience those that affect the aspects of life necessary to them.

For that way they are living according to God's rules and no other.

But if they are affected by the lives and needs of others to endow upon them great qualities, they cannot fulfil what is needed to justify a quality of life according to their own needs.

Let it be now that you understand that God cannot proceed with your life for you and that you must live that to which you are attuned, if you are to realise a full and worthwhile life.

For it is by giving love that we formulate reason and that must not impede our judgement on a situation where one person may be helped, but a need to be of upset is of learning value, and they must learn to be worthwhile to this situation if they are to move on in life.

Let it be that you are resolute and worthwhile in your creating happiness. For it will not be right if you have given that which is worthwhile but it is not a correct choice.

Let it be that you evaluate the situation first and then give it a need to be restored if at first you realise the solution to be worthwhile to all parties.

But then if a need shows where there is a need to encounter difficulty it must be left and the giving of love shall not doom it to failure, but a learning process, for we are here to learn that of goodness and worth to our souls. And if it is to learn hardship then it is good to know that we are able to accomplish that. For goodness shows only if a need is given, and that cannot be if there is a way out of a situation and it is not right for us.

Let it be that you evaluate and give only that which is challenging to a life and not just a realising of capability with life.

Let it be you soon learn the difference.

P

Pleasure (Channelled 31 May 2007)

Key Points

- There is a need for pleasure in our lives. That is what life is about.
- Some days, God's love and all the fulfilment of our surroundings is all that can satisfy us.
- We also need enjoyable experiences that bring fulfilment to the mind and body.
- Mankind cannot remain attached to the fulfilment of expensive purchases. He must appreciate simple pleasures too.
- Many things are enjoyable if we allow them to be. Love is one.
- Everyone can know the pleasure of loving and being loved. It is always there if we need it.
- God's love is not the issue. We must love and fulfil others' lives as we do our own.
- Sharing helps us to feel good, and love makes us forgive and also serve others.
- God forgives, so must we.
- It is very necessary to love. Do not forget it.

- Love is a constant that carries you through distressing and unsettling situations.
- Love is a compelling part of your life. It will bring fulfilment when you need it.

A Clear Account

Jesus tells us in this writing that there is a need for pleasure for our lives are meant to be enjoyable. There are days that only God's love and our surroundings can satisfy our needs, but there is also a need for experiences we can thoroughly enjoy. This is a time when the body and mind are fulfilled totally, for the human race cannot rely only on the feelings that come from purchasing something expensive. Pleasure has also come from the simple things around us. The importance of these cannot be dismissed. Because we can enjoy many of the things around us if we allow it to happen and one of these is love. We can all enjoy that, both in giving and receiving it for it is always there when we need it. But God's love is not the issue. We must love to fulfil others as they do us.

The need to share love can make you feel good. It can also bring a need to forgive or serve others in a loving way.

You have to realise that because God forgives, He expects us to do so as well. For it is necessary to adjust to a more loving attitude. That is paramount and the need for it must never be forgotten, for the future can be miserable and unsettling, but love is constant and that can never change.

You must learn that love is a compelling part of your life. Even if you are sad or upset, love is there. It is there when you need it and it will bring you the fulfilment you require.

The Writing

It is good today to talk of the need for pleasure in our lives, for what else is life for but to be pleasurable?

Let it be that you see the full meaning of this statement, for there are days when we cannot take pleasure in anything except God's Love and that is all around us and able to satisfy us in the need given.

But there is also the need for pleasurable experiences; that we may fully commit the body and mind to a sensation of fulfilment and worth.

For the goodness of mankind cannot remain attached to that of purchasing goods and enjoying expensive fulfilment. It must come also from the simple pleasures that are around us and that cannot be dismissed.

For there are many things that bring us pleasure if we allow them. And the goodness of love is one of them. For we can all feel the pleasure of loving and being loved, for the pleasure is always there if we need it.

But God's Love is not the issue. It is necessary to be loved and to love those around us and fulfil their lives as we bring fulfilment to our own lives. And that need to share can bring us goodness felt. And that need to love can bring a need to forgive or to serve others through love also.

Let it be that you know now that God forgives and because He does we are expected to as well, for the need to adjust to a way of love is paramount, and that must never be lost, for the way forth can bring upset and unrest, but a need to be loved and to love is constant, and that can never change.

Let it be soon that you learn love is a compelling part of your life, and you cannot rid yourself of it, even if you are upset or unhappy. It is there and if you call on it, it will bring the fulfilment you need at the time you need it.

Pre-Life Choices
(Channelled 28 March 2007)

Key Points

- You make choices for your life according to your current need.
- You have continued to gain experience during your eternal life.
- You must complete this learning before you can serve others.
- Living your choices satisfies you and gives you a need to perform well according to your abilities.
- You are born with duties to perform.
- You build on your abilities.
- On whatever scale you are able to help yourself and others around you.
- Some serve God by causing upsets.
- Some are wicked so that they can resolve problems of crime and distressing situations.
- Some need to treasure the experience of loss.

- A child may experience things so that its parents learn the feeling of distress.
- Crime can bring opportunities for reform.
- It all reflects the Cause and Effect pattern of life.
- There is a need to serve God so that it brings reform and goodness to everyone.

A Clear Summary

Jesus says here that before you embark on your life you are given a particular need to fulfil during your life. You choose this need so that you can bring changes to your eternal life through which you have been gaining experience. You can choose a life of upset. It is up to you to choose what you need, and it is necessary education for you before you can work to serve others.

When you are born you bring duties to perform and you carry abilities that can be built on during your life. You need to perform certain tasks during this time and as each one is completed it will raise your level of worth, giving you an ability to help yourself and those around you, no matter how small or large the task.

There are those who have decided to serve God's purpose by bringing a variety of upsets. They may not have a wicked past but are to play a bad part in life so that it furthers the path of good. It may be that good has to be achieved at a price. The task may be to resolve crime and distress. Some need to cherish the experience of loss. A child may experience certain things so that parents can endure the feelings that brings. Crime may bring opportunities for reform. This all follows the Cause and Effect pattern of life. It is necessary to serve God in all ways that can bring reform and cultivate goodness in people's lives.

The Writing

You are given first a need to perform and that is chosen by you at your will so that you can bring changes to your eternal life or you can succumb to an upset if that is given to you to perform at will. It is your choice and you will choose according to your need at the time, for you will have been gaining an experience within your eternal life, which is necessary to complete before you can be of service to manifesting the needs of others within their need to perform. And that will bring satisfaction to the heart and a need to perform well in the capabilities of that manifested for you.

When you are born within a world to be of worth to duties to perform, you bring forth a capable approach that can be built on throughout life. It will bring you a need to perform certain tasks and it will bring a need to generate worth within the tasks given so that you are able to be of salvation to your own needs and to serve those of need around you, no matter how small or large.

There are people who have decided to serve God's purpose by bringing a need to serve an array of upset. They may not have led a wicked past but are to be of wicked approach in a need to implement a need to further a path of good, so that it may be seen that good is to be maintained at a cost, and it may not all be of wicked approach but a need to resolve crime and upset within a land.

For some it is worthwhile to live a life of upset within a need to treasure the experience of loss. Within a child some experiences are given that are of upset to parents so they may experience the upset of fervour. And a crime set pattern may lay open opportunities for reform. Let it all be that this is an accurate portrayal of all that is to happen within life that is of a need to promote the Cause and Effect approach to life. Let it be that you bear witness now to a need to serve God in all ways sound that are of a need to reform worth and bring an approach of worth and goodness to all lives. Let that be all.

Progress Through Action
(Channelled 9 May 2007)

Key Points

- It is easy to achieve changes by prayer, but it is then tempting to pray more and lie back and do nothing.
- God needs you to progress in your life by learning new skills.
- You must follow God's worth. You can only satisfy some needs by enhancing your skills and worth.
- You learn and release the occasions when you failed to in the past.
- Be aware of your thoughts. As you wake or relax, things are in your mind to help you. Your mind repeats commands to you. You may see visions.
- Everything is there to power you on to learn more through books and joining groups.

- You voiced great choices before your life, you must now learn how to fulfil them and feel at peace with yourself.
- This is where you progress and it will be extremely worthwhile.
- Understand that God's policy is for you to enjoy seeing your dreams unfold, but you must play a part in the process.

A Clear Account

Jesus says that it is very easy to achieve such results through prayer that the temptation is to pray more and then lie back and let it happen. But this is not God's way, because he needs you to learn new skills and progress in the way you work as well as the way you behave with others. This will benefit you.

You have to understand that the future cannot arrange itself so that you can take off most of the time. You have to gain the fulfilment and ability to continue your progress. You cannot rest back on your laurels. It is not enough. You have to appreciate it is God's worth you are following and not your own. You can only satisfy some of the needs in your life if you gain more skills and worth. That is how you learn and let go of the times in the past where you did not learn.

Be aware of your thoughts and you will gain a lot of information. Listen to your mind repeating commands to you. These things are always in your mind as you wake, or at a relaxed moment in your day and at times you may be aware of visions that some people are afraid to see.

All this has to power you on to grow through reading books and learning generally. It can prompt you to join others and start bringing about change.

The learning must come and so must the action because you are bound by a need to physically commit to the great words you have when you made your choices. You chose your pathway and you must now learn how to fulfil it and feel the peace within yourself. This is where you progress and it will be immensely worthwhile. It will bring adventure and it will enable you to witness what is needed to help you.

You must understand that God's policy is for you to enjoy seeing your dreams unfold, and that can only happen if you take part in the process.

The Writing

It is easy to realise a prayer and be advantaged by it, so that it becomes a need to pray more and do less.

But it is not the way of the Father. For it is to advance capability and advance the way you work and are among people, that you are advantaged.

It is necessary to bring to your thoughts, your mind a need to realise that the way forth cannot manipulate itself in a way that brings you ultimate leisure. It has to be that you generate a way forth that is able and worthy, for that will bring you satisfaction and an ability to move on.

For that which went before will not satisfy if it is to be that you advance, and therefore you must bring forth the realisation that it is God's Worth you follow and not your own, for you are to satisfy some needs during your life, and that will be done only by living with the need to generate ability and worth. It is by those needs that you learn, and forgive the past where you have not learnt, for you are able to channel an enormous amount of information if you are able to wake up and listen to your thoughts and your mind's repeating of some commands.

For they are always in your mind when you are awaking, or are relaxed or in a time when you see that which others are afraid to see, and that must power you on and begin your own ability to enjoy the need to read books and learn, and then to bring yourself to join others and bring about change. For you are about change, and the learning must come, as must the action.

For you are bound by a need to serve that which is of outstanding rhetoric that has been given by you at your time of choosing, for you have chosen your pathway, and it is for you to choose now to learn the way to fulfil it and be at peace with yourself.

For you are about to advance your need to serve, and that will bring you an advancement of great worth through adventure and witnessing that which is of need.

Let it be soon that you realise that God's policy is to bring you the fruition of your own dreams. And that can only be done if you are willing to partake in the way necessary to achieve that.

Question of Principles
(Channelled 7 June 2007)

Key Points

- By upholding God's Principles you will find fulfilment and worth.
- Many things bring pleasure.
- If a person enjoys love in their life they find fulfilment.
- There is a need to see things with love, find fulfilment in laughter, in the people and nature you see.
- As God is within everyone, there is imagination and worth to enjoy and it is more satisfying than anything of monetary value.
- Many need to learn inner joy and to do this they need God. God satisfies all aspects of their lives if allowed.

A Clear Account

Jesus speaks of the need for mankind to uphold God's Principles, saying that the future cannot bring fulfilment and worth without them.

He says that many need to learn as they are in the grip of a materialistic society, and they cannot find fulfilment in that way. He adds that God's pleasures are everywhere, and man can find immeasurable fulfilment through love. If he did he would appreciate so much more than if he chose materialism.

Jesus encourages you to focus on everything and everyone with love, so that you can be fulfilled beyond measure. Each laugh, every person or animal would fill you with pleasure. God lives within everyone so there is imagination and worth beyond anything money can buy. So be satisfied with the love you feel and pass on your love to others so that they learn its importance too.

They need to learn that joy and they need to find God within themselves to appreciate it. For they are so caught up in generating money, that they have overlooked that greater prize of worth that will satisfy all areas of their life if they allow it.

The Writing

It is necessary now to write on the need to formulate a way forward that brings faith to mankind and an upholding of God's Principles, for the way forward cannot bring fulfilment and worth if it has not principles within it that are worthwhile. And that of the need now is to teach fulfilment and worth to all people. For they are held in the grip of a materialistic society, and that need now is to bring to them a need not to hold such materialistic values above and beyond the need for fulfilment.

For there are many things that bring us pleasure and it must be that these are seen for the goodness they hold within. For God's pleasures are manyfold and they may be seen and felt everywhere if they may be given that opportunity to serve.

For where else would there be fulfilment if a man held to a need to generate worth within a life, and he held only to the pleasure of love? For there would be fulfilment in his day and beyond, for there would be many things that he would see, that he cannot if he chooses only materialism.

Let it be that you adjust your vision so that you see all around you with love and then you will be fulfilled beyond measure. For there would be fulfilment in every laugh, each bud on every tree would bring pleasure, and every animal or person that you saw would fulfil you.

For the living of God within everyone brings an imagination and worth held beyond the countenance of all that that satisfies only monetary value.

Let it be that you are satisfied soon with the love you feel that endows all people with a need to generate that love also. For they are of need to learn that which is joy within, and they shall not feel it until they are redeemed by the love of God's Worth.

For they are not formulated by love, but hold within a need to generate money and they must learn that within there is a greater prize of worth and that it shall satisfy all aspects of their life if they let it.

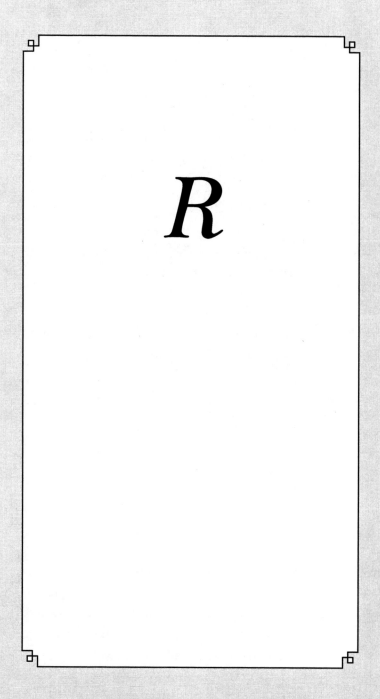

R

Relationships (Channelled 15 June 2007)

Key Points

- There are some who think only of themselves. Some others in relationships feel they are always right, whether or not it is true.
- People like these need to generate love within a relationship. Discontented with life they only bring unhappiness.
- Some are not physically violent but abuse others' minds and characters.
- This is as bad as physical violence as it leaves the victim feeling worthless if not ill.
- There is a need to build up people's characters and not demolish them.
- If you are affected by this abuse do not allow it to hurt you.
- You are a child of God. You have God's gifts and the ability to change and find happiness again.
- If you are an abuser of people's spirits, you need to restrain from it. The more you carry on the greater the need to address it.

- The resolute worth of God will bring you an invigorating and worthwhile future if you allow it.

A Clear Account

This writing from Jesus says that some people are selfish and think only of themselves, whilst others always feel they are right and never believe otherwise.

People in these relationships need to generate love because they are discontented and that does not bring calm and resoluteness. It brings unhappiness.

Many will not resort to physical violence but they are as bad because they mentally abuse those close to them so that it affects both the mind and the character of the person involved. This can really upset the victim, and it can make some ill. That cannot be if they are to feel alert and well. They need to generate a future that is character forming, not character assassination.

So if you are affected by this do not allow it any longer. Refocus your mind. You are a child of God. Have faith in all the gifts that He has given you. They will help you to rebuild your character so that you are happy again.

If you are an abuser of people's mental and spiritual state, you need even more to practice restraint. The longer you continue the greater the need to restrain yourself. Allow instead for God's resolute worth and you will find the result is both invigorating and worthwhile, and you will not need upset. Learn this soon and change your life.

The Writing

Let it be we talk now of a need to generate love within the clandestine relationships held in the world. For there are those who think only of themselves and no others, and there are those who feel they are right within a relationship, whether they are or are not.

Let it be that they need to bring to one another a need to generate love, for they are ill content with life and will bring only unhappiness where the need shows for a calm and resolute worth.

Let it be that you understand now that many people cannot commit themselves to a life of violence but they are abusive in a way that is violent to the mind and character of a person. Let it be that they are no better than the ones of violent nature, for they leave an imprint on the mind of a person that will bring about a demolition of the worth of that person. And it will make them an upset and irritated person. For they who are irritated enough become ill, and that cannot be if we are to be alert and well in all aspects.

Let that of thy need now hold to generating a way forth that is of character forming and not demolition. Let it be that you adjust that which is in your mind if you are affected by this and allow it not to irritate or upset you.

Rest (Channelled 7 June 2007)

This is a formula for health and wellbeing.

Key Points

- There is a need to rest fully.
- There should be a day of rest, preferably at the end of the week.
- You should adjust your programme of work so that it includes rest.
- There is a need for both the body and mind to replenish.
- You cannot be alert to all things if you are tired.

A Clear Account

In this writing Jesus says that we need a day of rest if we are to benefit fully in our lives, and we should adjust our thoughts to include this because God needs us to.

Although many do not work on Sunday a large number do so in order to get an income, but they cannot live life to the full if they do not have time for replenishment.

There are also those who choose to work every day and this upsets the need for rest. The world cannot be formulated to run full time. You need rest and you will not benefit fully until you achieve this. You need to be sharp and alert for many things in life, and you cannot be if you are tired.

Instead, you should adjust your life so that it includes rest time even if it is not at the end of the week, because it will benefit you and your health.

The Writing

There is a need some days to be able to rest fully and we need that day of rest if we are to benefit fully.

Let it be that we adjust our thoughts to bring about a change in thinking that it is of worth to our mental factor if we rest just one day in full and wholeness.

Let it be that you adjust your programme fully so that you can serve God's need for rest. For there are many people who will not work on a Sunday, but there are many who are forced to do so in order to bring about a need for salary paid. And they cannot be of full character to their lives if they are given not the replenishment and worth needed to be of service to their bodies and minds. And yet there are many who choose still to work all days given, and this must be of upset to the need to rest. For the world cannot be formulated to run full time and all time, and yet there are many who would do this for they are of contract to do this.

Let it be that you are accurate to the thought that there must be rest within your life and you cannot benefit fully until this is done. For there are many aspects of life that have to be faced in full character worth and that cannot be if you are tired and not alert to all things.

Let it be that you adjust your life accordingly and bring some area of rest within your working time even if it cannot be at the end of the week. For there are some who are not able to take this time but they can be of worth to another day given. Let it be soon that you learn that this is beneficial and worthwhile to your health.

S

Satan's Role (Channelled 27 May 2007)

Key Points

- If we serve love in the world, love will follow and when that is so there cannot be hate in our hearts.
- When hate exists, it destroys good and can only bring distress.
- We can serve good and we can serve evil in life. We decide and that is then enforced so that it benefits our character.
- Good has been founded in bad in many areas of life. Creating love can hold back the force of evil.
- Some believe God is the only source of good. Some good also comes from Satan.
- Satan creates an offence to bring about change where it is needed.
- Sometimes it is necessary to highlight a cause. Satan recognises this and helps to rectify it.

- God's message is for peace, but Satan's is for change, rather than let the world endure distress.
- Some needs in the world are not discussed. They are too deep.
- God's value is paramount, but there is a need also for Satan to invoke change.
- God has to intervene in some things, but so does Satan.

A Clear Account

Jesus tells us here that we can bring about goodness and justice in our work serving God's values, because if we serve the cause of love, love will follow, and when there is that in the world we cannot hold hate in our hearts.

But if there is hate, it destroys good until there is only a way that is distressing to people.

For there is no rule in life that says we cannot serve good and evil if we wish. But we are the ones that decide that, and whatever decision we have made must then be enforced, so that it is worthwhile to our character.

You have to understand that there are many areas in life where good has been founded in bad. Where there is evil, it may be held back by the need to create love.

Some believe that God is the only source of good, but some good also comes from Satan. He has brought about change where it has been needed, and this has been done by causing an offence to be made.

Some believe he will not defy the love of God and in some aspects that is true, but there are also certain areas of need that lead to change, and where a person may need to live a totally bad life, another may need only to highlight a cause. That is where Satan helps. He will recognise what is wrong and take measures to rectify it.

Because the will of the people brings about the focus of change, and where a need is apparent, this will happen.

You must understand that God's message is for peace, but Satan's message is to bring about change rather than upset or distress in the world.

Some needs are known to the human race, but there are others that are deeper and these are not discussed. No-one is told about these because it is only necessary for people to know if there is a need to expand on the plan for good.

And that would bring everyone to the Temple of Worth so they could deliberate and bring about an all enveloping failure or success in the extreme. That cannot be discussed, but where necessary there may need to be change.

You must understand that without doubt God's value is paramount. But there is also a need for Satan's power, so that he can bring about change where it is necessary, and not a power upset that cannot be reversed.

You must see now that there is a need for God's intervention in some things, but there is also a need for Satan's too. There are needs on both sides and that will bring change on Earth and as a result everyone will benefit.

The Writing

When there is love in the world, there cannot be hate in our hearts. For we are to be of service to love if there is that to follow, and we can bring about right and good in our work to be of God's values.

But if there is hate, there is a need to deflagrate such good to a way of upset and that cannot be.

For there is nothing in life that says that we cannot be worthwhile to good and evil if we wish. But we are the force that requires a decision, and where that decision is made, it has to be enforced in a need to generate that which is worthwhile to our character.

Let it be that you understand now that there are many areas of life where there is good that has been founded in bad, and that where there is an evil force there can be restraint, and that force may not succeed through the need to generate love.

For there are some who believe that the force of good only comes from God. But there are some forces of good and worth that come also from Satan.

For he has brought about change where there has been a need, and has invoked a principle of worth where there has been offence given.

For there are some who believe that he will not defy the Love of God and that is true in some aspects, but there are needs also that lead to change. And whereby man may survive fully on the need to create bad, there are some who will fulfil a need only to highlight a cause and that is where Satan helps. For he will set about in recognition of the fault and bring about the need to rectify it.

For it is the will of the people that endows a great force of change and that will be brought about if a need shows.

Let it be that you understand that God's message is for peace, but that the message given by Satan is to bring about change and not upset in the real world.

For there are some needs known to man but there are also those that are deeper and unspoken. And of these we tell no one for the need shows to tell only if we are needing to expand our plan of good. And that need shall bring all people to the Temple Of Worth in deliberation, and shall bring about extreme failure or extreme success. And that cannot be discussed but may merit a change in many things where it is necessary.

Let it be that you understand now that God's value is paramount and of that there is no doubt. But also there is a need for Satan's power so that he may bring about change where needed and not an upset of power that is of irrestorable value.

Let it be that you understand fully the need for God's intervention in some things, and also for the need to have Satan intervene also. For there are needs on both sides and that shall bring change and worth to all who live on the Planet Earth.

Scientology (Channelled 15 June 2007)

Key Points

- Many in the world are confused about the Scientology cult.
- Many are upset by it including those who are instigating upset within the alliance.
- The alliance is a business that is worthwhile to some and not others. There is no consideration for what is right and resolute.
- It is a powerful consolidate and the organisers who generate money are direct in the way they work.
- Those who oppose Scientology's need for force and frankness cannot understand the upset they experience because of their dislike for it.
- Scientology is a cult of great power and is not allowed to practice in the name of Jesus Christ. But it has practiced in that name and by using the authority of God while it delivers abuse and hate to the world.

- I (Jesus) do not approve and do not give authority for my name to be used where it involves hate and upset.
- Follow the Lord Jesus Christ according to his worth and not through an upsetting authority which is worthwhile to some and not others.
- Wherever a cult of evil intent practises it is not representing God.
- Scientology wants anarchy of faith so that those at the top benefit in any change to the world's faiths.
- I (Lord Jesus Christ) will not be of salvation to those stockpiling a fortune in the name of God.
- Bring changes to ban the cult from practicing within God's faith.

A Clear Account

Jesus begins this writing by saying that talking about the Scientology cult will upset many people, for many are confused by it and some feel it should be banned.

He says that many are upset by it including ones who have prompted concerns within the alliance. It is not one made in hell, but the business is worthwhile to some and not others and it is not considered necessary to include what is right and resolute. It is a powerful consolidate with direct people acting as organisers responsible for generating money.

Because some dislike the cult and oppose the force and the frankness that is shown, they suffer trouble and they do not understand this.

You can be sure in your own mind that this is a very powerful cult, and it must not divert the power of God's work by launching such authority on the world. It is not allowed to practice in the name of Jesus Christ; however it has done for some time. It has also held in the authority of God and yet it malpractices in some areas of work and that then brings abuse and hate to the world.

Jesus says that it is a formula of which he does not approve and that he has not authorised his name to be given to that which involves hate and upset within the glory of mankind. He adds that you should follow his instruction to be faithful to the Lord Jesus Christ according to his values and not by the degradation of an authority that is upsetting and is organised by mankind so that some are worthwhile to God but not others.

Many hide their fears and are bound by the operations of the cult of Scientology, but there are many who are caught up in the mania because of the distress created towards any who puts down the workings of the cult. It is necessary to understand that wherever a cult is practiced that is of evil intent, it is not worthy to God. Scientology's need is to create an anarchy of faith so that if a dispute looms which brings changes to the world's faiths, their top people will be in a very favourable position.

Jesus continues by saying that in no way will he bring salvation to people who intend to greedily stockpile fortunes in the name of God, and he says that you must bring about the necessary changes so that this cultish activity is banned from the practice of upsetting in the name of God.

The Writing

It is necessary now to write about the cult that is of Scientology and it will be a measure that is of force unto upsetting many people. For there are many in the world who are of disarray unto the Scientology faith that is practiced by some and who some feel are to be banned from the streets. For there are many who are upset by it and it is upsetting too to those who are the instigators of upset within the framework of the alliance. For it is an alliance not made in hell but it is of an attitude that that which is right and is resolute is of need not unto their need to carry on business. And that of the need now is to generate a business of great worth to some and of obverse choice to others.

Let it be that you are accurate in your thinking that this is a powerful consolidate and that the ones who organise and are responsible for the generation of money are attitudinally direct in their work. Let it also be said that the ones of worth who oppose the need for such force and such frankness cannot see merit in the upset caused to them when they are of obvious aversion to the cult.

Let it be that you are accurate in your mind now that this is a cult of great power and must not deviate the power of God's work into an infantile upset due to the launch of great authority on to the world.

Let it be that it is allowed not in the name of Jesus Christ to practice but it has held in the name and the authority of God's worth for some time, although it malpractices some of the efforts shown towards some of the work given that can deliver only abuse and hate to the world. For it is a formula of which I approve not and I hold in authority that my name not be given to that which involves hate and upset within the glory of mankind.

Let it be that you now follow my instruction to be of faith unto the Lord Jesus Christ as he is given by worth and not by the degradation of some upsetting authority set by mankind for the upsetting practice of authorising some to be of worthiness to God but not others. For there are many who consume their fears and are bound by the workings of the cult of Scientology but there are many who are held captive by the mania of some who will wilfully upset all those who are of derisory terms unto their practice.

Let it be that you understand now that no matter where a cult is practiced, if it is of evil intent it is not of worth to God, and that of the need for Scientology is to bring about an anarchy of faith so that there are those at the top who will be well favoured if a dispute looms and brings about a change to the needs of the world's faiths.

Let it be that you understand now that in no way shall I be of salvation to the ones of need who loom forth with greedy intent to stockpile their fortunes in the name of God.

Let it be that you adjust to this and bring about the change necessary that this cultish activity may be banned from the practice of upset within God's faith held.

See the Good in People
(Channelled 18 May 2007)

Key Points

- Not everyone sees good in themselves.
- Some do not want to appear loving and caring and so God formulates their characters accordingly.
- Some do not see goodness in others and if it is not evident they assume it is not there.
- It is necessary to see the good in all people and encourage it to grow.
- Some people are dull and miserable while others are gifted and lively. You should see the good in all of them.
- Help others to find satisfaction and to show goodness. It will help you too.

A Clear Account

In this writing, Jesus says that it is good when you know you are worthwhile as a person, but not everyone does even though they give of themselves totally.

He says that they work to God's principles but they don't enjoy the fulfilment that they would if they felt God close.

They have chosen not to show love and so this is how they come over as people, because not everyone wants to bring love into the dimension.

As a result, you have to learn that not all people are the same. Some are good but don't want to appear it. But having said that, they are willing to learn.

On the other hand there those who do not look for the good in others. They suspect that because there is no visible sign of it that it doesn't exist. Yet that is wrong. There are many who will do good things if they are given encouragement to do so.

So that is why it is right to believe everyone has good in them, and help them to generate that good, because they are giving themselves and, once they are given the right reason to be worthwhile, they will be.

Everyone needs to learn that there are those who tend to be miserable and always upset about something, whilst others are full of life and very capable.

To live as God needs, you must recognise the good in everyone and help them to believe in their own goodness. It will enable them to feel satisfied and become more generous in their manner.

It will also make you look more for the good in people, treat them well and, as a result, bring more fulfilment to your own life.

The Writing

It is good to realise that you are worthwhile as a person, but it is not always so. For you may give of yourself fully and not believe that you are a worthwhile person.

What you need is to realise that there is a way forward for those who feel like that and they are not abandoned. For they are of faith to God's principles but are not of wisdom to His presence.

For He may formulate that which is character forming and bring not the principle of love to the fore if the one who demands it is affronted by their need to love, and they cannot do it.

For it is a need of everyone not to bring love into the dimension, and although they are of goodness built they are willing to learn that which is of good intent.

Let it be that you learn now that all people do not hold within a dimension to be wise to the goodness of others, and they suspect that where there is no motive there is no need for fulfilment. And that is wrong for there are many people who will give goodness if they are met with kind intent and worth.

Let it be that you understand a need now to give all people that appreciation of being good so that they realise a need to generate good worth.

For they are giving of themselves, and they will be capable if they are given the right need to be worthwhile.

And it is a learning time for all people. For there are those who are morose and upset, and there are those who are gifted and lively.

Let it be that you see merit in all people and help them to believe that they are good and worthwhile in life.

For it will bring them satisfaction and the need to bring a little more generous attitude to the fore. And it will bring you a need to search more and bring an attitude of goodness held to all whom you meet so that they are worthwhile to your needs in full.

Serve God (Channelled 15 May 2007)

Key Points

- To serve God is paramount in our lives.
- We are God's children. By working lovingly we create a worthwhile life according to His principles.
- Live by God's values. They must apply.
- Many do not live by God's values. Their lives would be more enjoyable if they did.
- Be worthwhile in your life. Worth is given by God and you need to generate that value in your life.

A Clear Account

Jesus says that serving God in our lives is a prime need and everyone should understand that.

We are all God's children. We create a worthwhile life by working in a loving way on a project that falls within the boundaries of God's principles. This is where we work and we must consider our quest carefully so that we plan our life to run well within the needs of God.

Do this and live by God's values. For His Principles must apply and they allow your values to be judged. For many do not live by God's values and if they did live more rationally and completely they may feel better.

Be worthwhile in your life because you are given that ingredient and that must mean something if you are to plan something worthwhile. For worth is only given by God and you need to generate that value in your life.

The Writing

There is a need to serve God that is paramount in our lives and that must be understood.

We are all God's children and we generate worth by giving love to a project held to good within God's principles.

For it is within these principles that we must work and we must bring forethought to our quest so that we may plan fully for the need to survive in the goodness measured by God.

Let that of your need be to fulfil His purpose and live by God's values. For the rejuvenation of God's principles must abound and they will bring a judgement of the values held.

For there are many people who do not live according to God's values, and they may feel much better if they are given that need to live fully and rationally.

Let it be that you generate worth in your life because you are given worth to live and that must signify something if you are to devise a plan that is worthwhile.

For you are given a need to generate worth and that can only be given by God.

Shutting Out God
(Channelled 4 June 2007)

Key Points

- A lot of people do not want to be worthwhile to God, or include Him in their lives.
- Their rational thinking and independent needs fail to see a benefit.
- Many see ultimate value in items they purchase.
- They must learn to create love.
- Love is paramount if a life is to be worthwhile.
- Love is worth more than anything.
- It is God's Worth.

A Clear Account

Jesus says here that something that upsets a lot of people is the need to be worthwhile to God. Many do not want to include Him in their lives. They rationalise and in their need to be independent they fail to see a benefit in following that route.

Many think an expensive statue in the hall is of most value to them. But if they are to behave well to God, they must learn to create love. It is important. To make a life fully worthwhile then love is paramount. It must be held in esteem, because any love given is of value to God.

It is worth more than anything.

The Writing

It is necessary now to talk of those things that generate upset among many people, and that is a resistance against the need to be worthwhile to God, for there are many people, who are resistant to the idea that they must bring God within their lives. For they are people who are best described as those who need rational behaviour and an independent attitude, and that need to generate worth towards God's behaviour is not accepted as needed, for there are many who justify their lives by giving their all to a statue in the hall that means nothing but a price ticket. And that cannot be if they are to be of real behaviour to God, for they are to serve God in their need to generate love and that must not be diminished, for the need to generate love is important and it must be given a full importance if it is to bring a full worth to life.

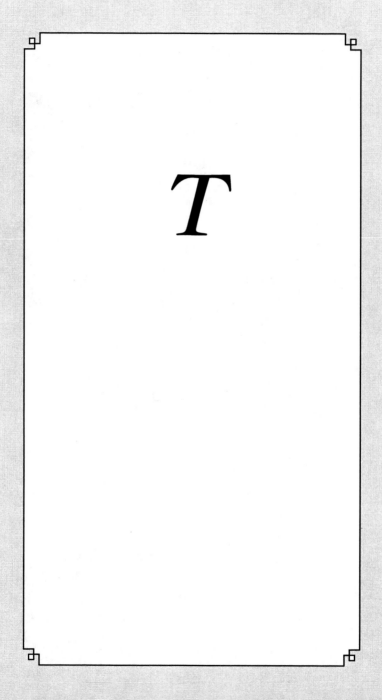

The Need to Generate Love
(Channelled 16 May 2007)

Key Points

- You find fulfilment by giving out and receiving love in your life.
- The principle of love needs your full attention whether it is to recognise the presence or lack of fulfilment.
- All people should see the value of living in love. They have what it takes if their attitude is right.
- Everyone has the power of love.
- There is a hate process which is less worthwhile, and unless it is particularly required, this is prohibited.
- Giving of love changes a person's character.
- It is beneficial to become a loving person. It they do not have the ability to communicate love is lost, and the result is no satisfaction or value to life.

- If you can give love you can also receive it. If you cannot give love you do not have the formula within to receive it.
- Positive thinking brings necessary changes to the formulae.
- Understand the techniques and use them fully.

A Clear Account

Jesus tells us in this writing that it is always necessary to give out and receive love during your life because it is by accepting these changes are needed that you find fulfilment.

Because people have to appreciate love and pay full attention to it, for sometimes you can see how fulfilling something is, and other times there may be a need for some.

Not everyone will see the need to live in love, but they ought to because they have what it takes, but if their attitude is not right it will not happen.

You must understand that everyone has the power to love. There is a process for hating too but that is less worthwhile, and unless there is a situation that demands it, it is prohibited.

You must see that a person's character changes through giving love. They find the ability to communicate in a more worthwhile and loving way. They do benefit if they can bring that change, but otherwise there will be such a drastic turnaround in their lives that they will be unable to communicate love, not even in thought.

As that magnifies they lose any feeling of satisfaction or value. And that is crazy, because giving love enables you to also receive it, but not giving it will prohibit your receiving it because it will not form up positively for you.

You must understand that positive thinking brings necessary changes to these formulae. So learn them soon and use them fully.

The Writing

It is necessary always to give and receive love in life, and it is willingness to bring about these changes that will fulfil a person.

For they need to evaluate the principle of love and give it their full attention. And that may be necessary because there is fulfilment to be seen or because there is a need for some.

For not all will evaluate and live in love, but they ought to for they are given all the equipment and need to love, but it will not do if the right attitude is not there.

Let it be that you understand that there is a power given to everyone and that is love. And there is a hate process too, but that has less worth to it and therefore prohibits the use of hate unless there is an issue that directly needs it.

Let it be that you understand now that a giving of love brings about changes in a person's character, and they are able to communicate love and worth more easily.

If they are able to bring about the change they will benefit but if not they will bring about a change so drastic in their lives that they are not able to communicate love, so there is little principle in it held to forethought. And that magnification of unreal worth brings about a lack of satisfaction and worth held to their person.

And that can be a crazy act, for if you are able to give love you are able to receive it also. But if you are not able to give love it is not possible to receive it either for it will not formulate in a way positive.

Let it be that you understand that positive thinking brings about changes needed to these formulae.

Let it be soon that you understand fully the techniques used and use them fully.

The Work Place
(Channelled 18 June 2007)

Key Points

- There is a great deal of aggravation in communities including business communities.
- Business cannot operate for money alone.
- Employers should create a caring working environment.
- Many workers only receive the fulfilment of getting paid for their work. They do not receive care and consideration from their employers.
- When care is part of the package an employee is happy to respond with more effort.
- A caring environment would bring value to the workplace instead of disagreements and a consuming dislike for the people in charge.
- Given a choice, many would leave an uncaring environment.
- It is necessary to bring changes so that good is seen in the work place.

A Clear Account

Jesus says here that we need to generate more love within communities and those he refers to are places of work. He says that although businesses have a need not to fail, there is such a need to generate money that it creates hate in the workplace.

Many hardworking employees receive only money as their reward and yet if an employer were to have a more caring attitude to the workforce they would find that they would put in more effort too, and this would have the knock on effect of making it a better place to work and not one where there is a consuming hate for the people in charge.

You should be aware that although many enjoy their work, they would gladly leave if the choice were there, because there is no caring attitude or inner reward felt.

This should be changed quickly so that the workplace becomes a good place and not an upsetting one.

The Writing

It is today we talk about the need to generate love within communities. For there is much aggravation in the community and it cannot base its need for love on anything but a need to generate business and above all, make money. For it is fortuitous not to fail as a business, but there is a level when those who are employed need the caring attitude of an employer and not to generate hate in the workplace.

For many are fastidious in their work and yet they are given nothing for it but money, and yet if they were given a higher value like the caring attitude of an employer they would bring around their need to serve so that it fulfilled all and gave each one a need to generate more as well. And it would bring the formula of worth to the workplace instead of upset and devouring hate for the ones in charge.

Let it be that you are aware that many people enjoy their work but not the place of their work, and if they are given a choice they will abandon the need to work within a framework where there is no love or goodness seen. Let it be that this is adjusted soon and a need given to convert that of upset to a need to be of worth to good.

Total Wellbeing
(Channelled 7 June 2007)

Key Points

- We need a wellbeing that creates calm within us.
- We lead hurried lives and we even eat quickly.
- It is better to eat smaller portions and eat slowly without snacking.
- Many people are too heavy and do not have a feeling of fulfilment.
- Unhealthy eating leads to disorders of the stomach and the system in general.
- There are too many chemicals in food which adversely affect the brain and the body.
- Our bodies are mainly made up of water and a high chemical intake can have a strong impact on our bodies and brains.
- We should eat mainly organic food.
- We should not eat more than necessary.

A Clear Account

Jesus says here that God needs us to have calm in our lives but too often our schedule is hectic and meals hurried. The need for a healthy lifestyle cannot be achieved for several reasons. It is better to eat less, eat slower and stop snacking between meals. In that way you can achieve better weight and a healthier life.

Many people are heavier than they need to be and they cannot feel fulfilled and happy unless they change their lifestyles. If they do they will feel the benefit.

Man cannot live by love alone but he cannot live by fat alone either. Unhealthy eating brings on stomach disorders and upsets to the system in general. But one of the most upsetting aspects of our eating is that of all the chemicals we consume. These affect the brain and the body. One of these effects is depression. Conflicting chemicals upset us. Our bodies have a high water content and chemicals that are carried within this affect our brains and our bodies. That leads to poor health.

You should instead eat mainly organic food and then only smaller portions and in that way you will bring a worthwhile formula to your life.

The Writing

It is necessary to talk of the need to give our thoughts to a wellness within that shall be brought about by our need to be calm, for we are made up of many factors and that which we hold within can bring about change within our limbs and our mind and within our need for peace and calm.

It is God's principle that we hold within a calm and serene approach to our lives, but that need now is to be of haste and upset and a lot of what we eat is eaten in haste too

Let it be that you adjust your lifestyle that you are able to bring about the changes necessary to your life that affect your body and your mind, for there are many aspects of life that do not bring goodness to your body, and it cannot be if you are to live a healthy life. It is better by far to change your lifestyle than to abandon the right to a happy and healthy life. For the need now is to eat more slowly and abandon the need to snack, but allow for smaller portions and less on your plate.

For you are of need to adjust to a lighter lifestyle and that shall be obtained by reaching a better weight and lifestyle than is common with most. For there are many people who are heavy beyond their need and they must bring about change if they are to attain that of fulfilment within, for they are needed to lose weight and become healthier in their life frame, for they will feel the benefit and see the difference within life.

For it is given that Man cannot survive by love alone and it is a fact, but however much he tries he cannot live by fat either. For there is a need to cut down much of the unhealthy eating that leads to disorders and upsets of the stomach and the system in general, for there are many things that affect our lifestyle and we must be

aware that by eating too much or too often we are upsetting our systems.

But we are unaware of the aspect that brings most
upset and that is the aspect that holds to generating too
much substance in the brain that brings about a need
to be morose and upset in behaviour. And that need is
brought about in many cases by the unreal worth of
all the chemicals we consume now, for there are many
within the brain and also within the body that affect our
balance of worth, and that must be altered if we are to
face the world with authority and worth.

For the way cannot be formulated within a need
for chemicals and they cannot bring worth to our lives
in fulfilment of our brain's needs if we are to consume
too many of the conflicting types, and yet we are given
them in great quantities within our lives and we consume them with vigour. For they will remedy our need
for upset but will instil a need to generate more formulae and upsetting aspects.

For it is given that our bodies are mainly of water
and if they are given then to be full of chemicals within
that water, it will instil into them a dynamism that con-
trols not only the brain and power held in a fulfilling
way, but in a compelling way that affects our thoughts,
our mind and beyond that in our bodies too. Better to
be aware that there are many factors that cannot help
us but bring about upset instead.

Let it be that you formulate your life according to the
need to eat that which is of mainly organic worth and
bring not a need to consume more than is necessary, so

that your body's worth will be of better proportion and worth than you have known before. Let it be soon that you try this and bring a formula of worth to your life.

U

Ultimate Choice
(Channelled 10 May 2007)

Key Points

- We alone have the choice between being good or evil.

- We choose before we embark as people within this life.

- We can choose to be good or part good and part bad.

- It is necessary for our spirit to experience evil thinking and behaving badly during its eternal life.

- We are all connected in spirit and through this connection, if it is necessary a higher authority will decide on an evil action for us to perform.

- Some people will be purely evil if results can be achieved earlier.

- Good alone cannot always bring benefit in the world. Sometimes there has to be some bad in the formula.

- No one benefits from all good. It cannot hold a distinction unless there is a contrast with bad.
- Where there is bad, there is an equal and opposing force of good.
- There is a dominant force of good in the world.
- If God intervenes an evil force must succumb to good.
- This is the formula by which man exists.
- Man will remain a dominant force as long as he commands good in the world.
- The need to destroy will end soon.
- Some adhere to the old formula of good and bad, and this will grow until there is no longer a need for it.
- The formula will end and there will be happiness and worth in the world as God intends that anything that is not good will finish.
- People will live simply and well in a joyful and blessed world.
- Not all men need good, but evil cannot rule. It helps some who live through it and realise that good is better.

A Clear Account

Jesus explains here that we alone have the choice between being good or evil in life. We choose our pathways before we live our lives here on Earth and part of that choice is between being a good or bad person.

If it is good, that is a single value to live, but we may choose a mixture of values to experience and that is more difficult. We cannot choose to be fair if we also want to be unfair.

Our pathways are found while we make our choice and it depends on whether we need to fulfil a good or evil experience. It is not always possible to choose good because we must experience evil thinking and behaving badly as a part of our spirit life.

We are all connected in spirit. And if we can all communicate in the case of something big, a higher being may dictate evil action. It provides the formula for others to follow, because if by being completely evil a result can be achieved sooner, this will be done.

For there are many ways to achieve results through God's formula and good cannot always achieve the best results unless there is an element of bad within it. No one benefits if it is only good. There must be a visible contrast with bad.

In any case, evil must succumb to good if God intervenes. For that is how mankind is made and the human race will remain dominant as long as it commands good in the world.

It is important to teach that which is of ultimate choice, because we have the choice between good and evil. And that must be our choice and not for anyone else to choose. For the need to destroy is coming to an end soon, which will please many people. Yet some will adhere to the old formula of good and bad and it will succour and grow for a while until the need for it ends.

Not all people need good, but where there is bad, there is an equal and opposite force of good, so evil cannot take control. However it does enable some to experience living through evil and understanding the benefit of a force that is primarily good.

The Writing

It is for us to choose our pathways before we become people in this life. And that need then also brings a choice between good and evil. For we have both to choose from, but it is only one of good that can be chosen if it is to be a single worth we feel. But if it is a multitude of worths chosen and we are then to choose between an evil part and a good part, then it is more difficult.

For we are not able to choose a fair life if we are to be unfair. And yet that is a choice open to us if we are to favour the popular vote.

For it is in our choosing that our pathways are sought, and it is in that need to fulfil all that is good or bad in a situation that brings us to a point of choosing whether we will play a good part or an evil part in the making.

For it is not always possible to opt for good as it is a necessary part of our lives in spirit to experience that which is of evil thinking and an unreal worth.

Let it be that you understand now that we are all connected in spirit, and if it can be decided that we shall all communicate together for the message is big, then it must be that at times there is to be one of higher worth that dictates an evil doing.

It formulates the way for all others to follow so that some may be seen to be better and get better results, and there are those who would solely be evil if they can achieve the results sooner.

For there are many ways to achieve results in the workings of God's formula and it must be seen that the way of good cannot always achieve that of goodness unless there is a factor of bad that is attached to it.

For it will benefit no one if the need is only to be good, and it will bring no one a formula of great distinction if it is not seen in the contrast of a bad deed. For whatever is given to be bad there is an equal and opposing force of good. And so that a need shows for there to be a dominant force of good, there is an even greater force held to good than to bad. And even if these understandings were not known, an evil force would have to succumb to good if the formula of God intervened.

For that is the making of mankind. And he shall remain dominant in the world for as long as he is able to command a worth held to good.

For that need now to destroy is to be at an end soon, and that will bring favour to all those who seek it. And yet some will adhere to the old formula of some needing to do bad and evil things. And that formula will succour and grow for some time until the need shows to succour no more.

For the formula will end and all things will be of happiness and worth in the intent of God to bring all things that evade the notion of good to an end, and to supply instead that which is of worth to all. And to bring to all people that need to live simply and well in a world that is blessed and given that which is of simple joy.

Let it be soon that you realise that the needs of all men is not for good. But for all that is done for bad, there is an equal and opposing force for good, so that evil cannot command in the world but it can offer opportunity to bless a few who will benefit from the experience of living through evil and knowing that a better life exists if the worth is given primarily to good.

Understand Your Power
(Channelled 9 April 2007)

Key Points

- You are given your power at birth. You may either need to act with purpose in your life or you may need to take things slower.
- You need to adjust so that you serve the purpose of your work.
- You can generate more power if that is needed.
- There is an ongoing need to bring happiness and enjoyment to your soul for the next life.
- Without a need to serve a soul can remain dormant.
- May you be gifted in a way that sustains the soul and brings you a need to serve.

A Clear Account

Jesus explains here that your power is given at birth and you may require a life full of purpose or one you live at a slower pace, for that which is given can be restored when it is needed, or it can be left without. You have to adjust your life accordingly so that you serve the purpose of your life.

You can generate more power if long ago you held these desires and needs. In fact a need can remain until your next life so that your soul can fully enjoy the happiness and enjoyment given to it. A dormant soul must awake with a need to fulfil or else it will remain dormant with no secure or worthwhile future.

May you be gifted according to your need to serve so that it brings sustenance and worth to the soul.

The Writing

Your power is given to you at birth and you may instil in yourself a great need to be of purpose in your life or a need to resonate at a slower rate, for that given can be restored to a future pattern of need when it is shown it is needed than if it is given no need to grow.

Let it be that you understand fully the need to adjust your life fully to serve the purpose of your career set. Let it be known fully that you can give yourself a need to generate more power to your life fully met by the desires and wants of a need held long ago.

Let it be that you know that a need remains to be embodied in the next life that a way forward may be found to bring happiness and jubilation to a soul. For a dormant soul must awake to a need to serve else it be left dormant to be of no secure worth for the future.

Let it be that you are gifted according to your need to serve and that shall bring sustenance and worth to the soul

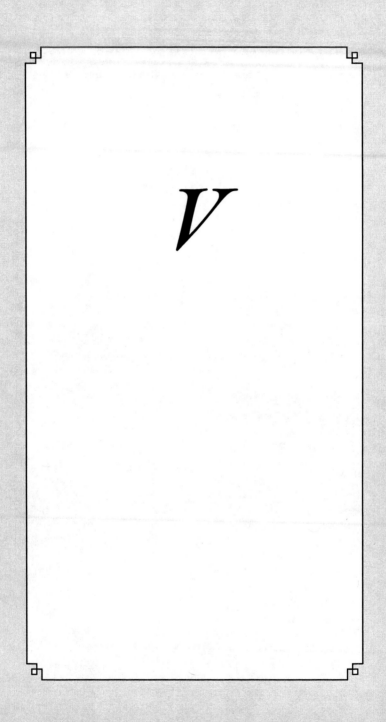

V

Valuing Older Workers
(Channelled 6 June 2007)

Key Points

- There is a need to allow people to continue a career after their sixtieth birthday.
- Excluding older workers is unnecessarily distressing.
- Many give their best and are dynamic after the age of 60.
- Older people could contribute to the nation's welfare if allowed to do so.
- Some younger people would enjoy more leisure and could learn to job share.
- Some young workers need to learn the job fully before becoming managers.
- Some older people are able to teach others to do a job.
- It is best everyone has an opportunity to learn and older people have the chance to pass on a wealth of information.

•   This should happen.

A Clear Account

Jesus endorses here the need to employ older people and says that it is not necessary to retire people when they are still able to do the job, and there is no need for it. For it upsets their spirit and can damage the way of life for all people if it is allowed.

There are many who give their best after their sixtieth birthday and if they want to work and are able, they should be allowed to. The rules that bring so much distress should be changed to include those who need to work after their sixtieth birthday but cannot. Because they are dynamic people in many ways and the apathy and upset that is created now must end.

For those people are not able to continue in their careers but they could pay tax and contribute to the nation's welfare if they were allowed. But they are not. They could also take over from some young people who enjoy leisure when they are given the chance. For some contribute little or nothing to the country's economy but will accept the benefits if they are unable to work.

However, they will learn, given the position that work must be shared and that means learning the job and contributing to it equally with others, so that they are on a level with everyone else.

It should be that they understand that certain areas of work must be taught fully and not left part done and completed later.

Mankind must adjust so that he recognises that there are some who need to learn their trade first, before taking on manager responsibility. But also there are older people who are able to teach and demonstrate to others how to master the job. So each in turn learns the work and passes on the information. In that way everyone had the opportunity to learn and adjust their lives, allowing the older people to pass in their wealth of information.

Hopefully this will soon happen.

The Writing

It is necessary now to talk of the need not to retire people early when they are able to conform to the work needed of a job.

Because there has been a legality drawn up that upsets those who are older and there is no need for it, for it will bring upset to the soul and damage the way of life for all people if allowed.

Let it be that there are many who give of their best after they are sixty and if they want to work it should be that they can for they are able.

Let it be that the rules that magnify upset shall be changed to include many who need to work on after their sixtieth birthday, but cannot. For they are dynamic people in many ways and that way which brings apathy and upset cannot be allowed to continue.

For they are able not to continue in the same career and yet they are able to contribute to tax and bring more money to the nation if they are allowed. But they are not because they are too old and that is unreasonable.

And they will be able to take over from many young people who will not be able to contribute the stamina but are able to enjoy leisure time fully if they are given the chance. For they are the ones who give nothing or very little to contribute to the country's economy, but they are willing to take the benefits offered if they are unable to work.

But they will learn, if given the stature, that a work-load must be shared and that given to them must be a need to learn work and give to it fully and equally with all men so that they may be of equal character to all others.

Let it be soon that they learn that there are areas of work that must be learned with full authority and not some that are to be left undone, but are able to be learned later.

For forthwith there must be some adjustment in mankind so that he can see that there are those who need to learn their trade first and then master the career ahead. But there are also those who are older and able to teach and show others how they may be of complete worth to their job. For they are able and are then able to teach that which they have learned and been given to pass on, so that all people have a chance to learn and adjust their lives, so that as older people they can pass on that magnitude on information to others. Let it be soon that they realise that this must be done.

W

Wealth (Channelled 19 June 2007)

Key Points

- Some people are fortunate in being able to make money and use it to help the world.
- Many do not believe money is easy to find. Some complain that they are not wealthy because they are not lucky. They are wrong. They cannot make a fortune unless they have the will to do what is needed.
- It is good to be wealthy. There are a greater number of people who complain about having to be poor than there are actual wealthy people in the world and yet they could be equal.
- When people's resolve is small towards becoming wealthy, their attitude is ineffective for making money. They need a growing mind that manifests and sees what is available to them.
- Money is available in the world wherever wealth exists.
- God's basic need for you is to be happy. If this involves wealth you must be able to achieve it.

- You must share your wealth so that the poor also benefit.
- Make sure you are one who benefits so that others can follow and wealth can spread and bring love to all who struggle and live in distress.
- Everyone is allowed to be wealthy but only a few help themselves to actually achieve it.

A Clear Account

Jesus says here that some are fortunate in their ability to make money, and they must use it to full advantage to bring about changes in the world.

Many people believe that money is hard to find, they tell themselves that the security is not there for them. They do not understand the purpose of money and so they see no way that it can provide fulfilment. Yet others possess a passion for making it and that is good if they commit to helping the world as well as themselves, because they enjoy making money and adopt the framework in their lives that will achieve it. Meanwhile others complain that they are not lucky and that is why they are not wealthy, but they are wrong. They cannot make a fortune if they do not have the will to do what is necessary.

You must understand that it is good to be wealthy. It is good for many people and provides advantages to most, so you are not helping yourself if you complain about not being wealthy. For many do get upset about having to be poor. There are more of these than there are wealthy people, and yet they could be equal if they were determined to change their lives and grow in stature. When their resolve towards wealth is small, their attitude makes them ineffective, but when they have an expanding mind that manifests and sees what is available, it becomes achievable. And throughout the world where there is wealth there is money available.

God's worth must be seen in everyone whether or not they are prosperous, but God's basic need for you is for you to be happy and if wealth is part of this it must be achievable. However the path you walk can only be paved with gold if you are resolved to sharing it, so you need to change your life so that you can share God's values and create financial freedom. Once you have done that, as well as making valuable changes for yourself, you must share your wealth so that the poor may be made better and so that God's love can be seen to surround all mankind and not just a part of it.

You have to value your life in such a way that you share goodness with everyone and so that all those who are in need can benefit. In that way, we will have given credence to this advantageous way that can only come with money. So few have the benefit so make sure you are one and then others can follow your example and money can spread and bring love to everyone who lives in stress without money. Let this happen soon in your life for everyone is allowed to be wealthy but only a few can help themselves to achieve it.

The Writing

It is necessary now to talk about wealth and the making of it, for it is fortuitous to some to have the skill and it must be that they use it to full advantage and bring about changes to the world.

Let it be that you understand that many people believe in the elusiveness of money, of that protection to the worth of someone. They are based on the frugal understanding of someone who has not the advantage of purpose, so they see no fulfilment in the basis of money. Yet some are able to locate a passion for making money and that is good if they are to be of worth to the world's needs as well as their own, for they are of true favour to the making of money and they compel themselves to adopt the right framework to bring about that stage.

Yet there are some who will not advantage themselves yet they complain that they are not well fortuneists because they are not the lucky ones. They are wrong, for they are not able to make a fortune if they are not willed to bring about the effort.

Let it be that you understand that it is good to be wealthy and that is of goodness to many people and of advantage to most so it is an attitude held disadvantage to complain when you are not wealthy. For there are many more who complain of a need to be poverty stricken than are wealthy, and yet they may be made equal if they resolve to bring about a change in their lives and that is to grow in stature. Where they have small minds of resolution to wealth they are attitudinally ineffective, but where they have a growing mind that manifests money, it is available to them. And that can occur throughout the growing area of the world, where there is wealth there is more available.

Let it be that you understand that God's Worth must be seen in all people whether they have wealth or are not wealthy, but the underlying need is to understand that God needs you to be happy, and if it is a need for wealth that is of virtue to your life it is necessary to achieve it. But it is resolute that the way forth can only be paved with a gold floor if the way of need is to be shared, and the need is to bring about changes that involve a great value to you. But the need is to share the wealth of God's values and bring about that financial freedom, and you may bring about changes that involve a great value to you but the need is to share that given so the poor may be made better, and the love of God is seen to surround all who inhabit the Earth and not just a few.

Let it be that you evaluate your life so that you may share goodness with all people and so that the way forth shall benefit all those in need. In that way you will have given credence to the fact that a way of advantage cannot be sought without the involvement of money. And yet it is an advantage given to few so benefit while you may and let others see the wisdom of the procedure you follow so that that of the worth of money can spread and bring love to all who encounter strife and upset in their lives and not the goodness of wealth. Let it be soon that you allow this to happen, for all people are allowed to be wealthy, but only a few can advantage themselves to be of worth to it.

Work Related Stress
(Channelled May 2007)

Key Points

- It is hard if you do not enjoy your work.
- Work at your relationships with fellow workers.
- Give your best if you wish to move on in your job.
- Sometimes you can change working conditions but not always.
- If you are bullied, face your tormentors or get colleagues to work with you to stop it.
- If you cannot enjoy your job, optimise your home time so it compensates.

A Clear Account

Jesus says here that it is hard if you do not enjoy your work, because it's a large part of many people's days. If it is a matter of not getting on with your colleagues, there is a limit to what you can do. If it is a job that fulfils you,

you are developing your skills, so maybe you need to work at your relationships with your fellow workers.

Maybe the working environment does not suit you, but you must continue to give your best if you are to move on. No one progresses by giving less than their best.

Maybe you are competent at your job but need better working conditions. Sometimes you can change this, but not always. However, you will help your case if you give your very best. When that happens and you are doing so well the present system cannot keep up, you may find that your managers realise and they change the system to accommodate you better. If this is a possible alternative then you should pursue it by complaining and requesting better working conditions.

If you are bullied, this must be stopped, and sometimes it can be by facing up to your tormentors and telling them what they are doing to you. You may have to do this through a tribunal, or you may prefer to take a gentler approach and ask them directly why they are bullying you.

If they behave properly, they will apologise and be polite in future, but if they are not and the situation is set to continue, you either have to take command of the situation if you are senior to them, or change your work. Because you have to feel good about what you do or it is not worthwhile. A third option is to tell your other colleagues about the problem and work together to stop the bullying from continuing.

It is good to enjoy your work, but that is not always possible. You then have to evaluate whether it is worthwhile continuing in the job or if indeed it is possible to leave it.

If it is not, you will have to be content with making your free time as good and empowering as possible to compensate for your working time, so that it makes your time at work more worthwhile.

The Writing

It is no good exercising our will to work if we are unfortunate enough to not get on with our colleagues. But this must be viewed with a degree of limitation, for we are limited in our choices of work and we must comply if we are to fully extend our capability.

Maybe you need to bring a little pleasure to your work by committing yourself to generate faith and worth in your relationships.

Maybe you are not suited to the work environment, but it will expect of you as you expect of it; a way forth that generates a command in your approach. And you must not give less than of your full if you are to revitalise the way needed.

Let it be that you are competent at your job and your need to bring changes to the environment level that you are working at.

Maybe it can be done and maybe it cannot, but it will help your cause if you are a prolific worker and that need to be worthwhile is causing an upset to the system.

For you will be seen to be worthwhile and there might be a need for the ones above you to generate a better circumstance for you.

If this is possible pursue it and allow yourself to be in the forefront of complaining and asking for better conditions.

Let it be that you are an upset person due to the bullying tactics.

This cannot be allowed to continue and it is necessary now that you face up to your colleagues or working partners and hold them responsible.

This can be through tribunal or you may want to generate a better worth felt by allowing those around you to give a sound basis for their bullying

If they are worthwhile they will say that they are sorry and be polite in the future, but if they are not they are going to be an upsetting influence fulltime to you and you will have to have a degree of authority with them that you have a stature above them or you hold a need to change the work you do. For the way forth cannot be happy if you are only able to maintain a degree of worth held and that cannot be so.

Alternatively, you can share with others around you and defy the upsetter by getting together an army of people who will not allow the upset to continue

It is good if you enjoy your work but you cannot always and if you need to change it must be a process of evaluation that tells you if this is possible.

If it is not you should be content with your work by being worthwhile to other things when you are off work for it will compensate and allow you a need to restore energy and combat the need to change work.

Working Together (Channelled 9th May 2007)

Key Points

- You have to work with others to achieve your dream. You cannot do it alone.
- Many have not learned to work together, and yet it is simple.
- To build a better future we must have others' help. They can bring courage and worth to the task.
- Companies are a 'company of people', of companions travelling the same route.
- Adjust your life. Others may have knowledge that is new to you.
- Build a worthwhile career for yourself. Share your knowledge and gain from others.
- Some are humble and survive together.
- Some are arrogant and that brings selfishness. They will not share power. This is not wise.
- Be wise. Share what you create.

- Divide the work with others and achieve together. It is progress.

A Clear Account

Jesus tells us that working together with others helps you achieve your dreams. You cannot do it alone. Many fail to progress because they have not learned to work with others and yet it is simple.

Some think they can do everything alone, they do not need others, but that is wrong. It is not possible. The future has to be adjusted if you fail to give and receive help, and that is no good if a pathway is to be clear and wise.

To build a better future we need other people's help. They can be worthwhile companions and bring courage and worth to the task. That is why we have the ability and reasoning to start companies. For that is what it is – a company of people, of companions travelling the same route.

So adjust your life accordingly because that then allows you to accept that someone else can walk alongside you. And that can be useful if you need to grow as an individual or in a way of serving the world.

Be strong in your career and be ambitious for yourself. For your nature is giving and that must bring you satisfaction. Share your knowledge and gain from others' knowledge. They will bring you a need to serve in new areas, and they will create a need within you to do more.

The Writing

It is important to collaborate with others to achieve your dream. You cannot do it alone. For there are many people in the world who are not able to venture forward in their lives because they have not learned to collaborate.

And yet it is a simple task. For there are those who think they can do everything alone. It is not for them to work with others. But they are wrong and it cannot be done.

For the way forward must be adjusted if you are to partake not in the realms of giving and receiving help. And that cannot be if the way forth is to be abundantly clear and wisely held.

To be of configuration to a better future is to bring the help of others to our side. For they are better held to be companions of worth, and they can bring great valour and worth to our need to perform.

That is why we hold the reasoning and ability to start companies. For that is what it is; a company of people - of companions travelling the same route.

And let it be you adjust your life accordingly. For the need to adjust brings forth an ability to mentally take in the knowledge that another person may serve alongside you, and bring you a knowledge that you are unaware of. And that may be a useful thing if you are needing to grow as a person, or in a service to the world.

Let it be that you are stalwart in your career, and give forth an ambition to generate a worthwhile future for yourself.

For you have a giving nature, and that must bring you satisfaction, so share your knowledge, and bring forth a need to gain from the knowledge of others, where appropriate.

For they shall bring you a need to serve where you have not trod before, and they will generate a worth within you that is good and feels worthwhile to the need to create more.

For where there are those who are humble, they need to survive and they can do this only by surviving together.

But where there is no humility, there can be arrogance, and that shall bring a need to generate only a wisdom for oneself, and not for others. For it is not a power to be shared. And then it is a poor wisdom. For it has not given that which is of need – a way forth that is of generating friendship and a co-existence of forces.

Let it be that you are wise and are one who will share that which you are creating, and not just one who is adamant about working alone and cannot share, and cannot bring about those things that are needed by dividing the work between others and achieving together. For that is the way forward.

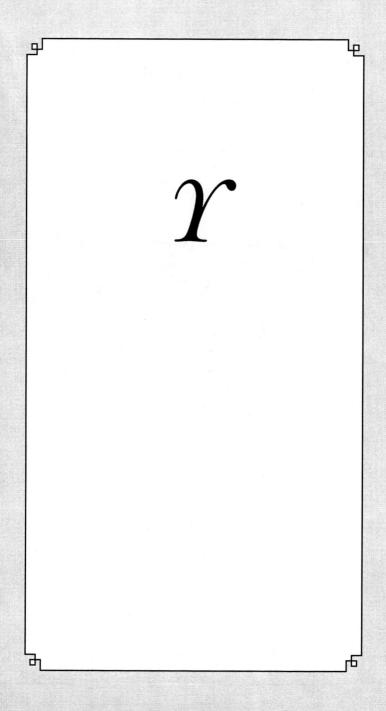

You Choose How Long You Live
(Channelled 10 May 2007)

Key Points

- Your life must have purpose. It will end if it has none because there is no need for it.
- If someone achieves a higher worth than anticipated and they need to fulfil that level they will live until that need is over.
- A person may endure, for instance, 6 months of pain and suffering to increase their level of worth in the spirit realms.
- Some who have not served God are unaware of their length of life until it is necessary to know.
- Some may suddenly realise their need to serve God and help themselves by doing more in the world.
- Suicide in not pre-planned and it is not recommended as an escape from suffering. It only brings a temporary change.
- Some murderers and those who commit suicide must face events again.

- Where the ending of a life is not pre-planned some players have to relive the type of situation again and make changes; those who murder have to be aware of their mistake and make recompense too.
- The giving of love commits all people to create that which is worthwhile.
- God provides what is necessary for everyone so that the values they apply give them a need to serve.

A Clear Account

Your life must have purpose. If it is without purpose it will end because there is no need for it.

If a person is given a long and worthwhile life to live and they achieve a higher worth than was anticipated they will live until the time needed is ended. By that time they will no longer have a need to stay.

A person may receive the power to withstand pain and suffering over a period of say six months so that it increases the level of their worth within the realms of spirit. They will have created themselves a better way forward through the learning of pain and upset. It taught them courage and that in turn helped them combat any illness in the mind. This allowed them to live that bit longer so that they could be successful in their learning.

Some do not know how long they will live until it is necessary. It may be that they have failed to serve God, and they have not been made aware of the fact yet, so they live a long and healthy life until it is necessary to be otherwise.

For those who do not have to succeed within a particular time can wake up to a new need to be worthwhile and find God. They suddenly realise their need to serve God and also to help themselves do more in the world.

Suicide is not pre-planned and it is not recommended as a way out of distress. Suicide can only bring temporary change to a person ending their life. They must relive the part of their life which they avoided so that they can overcome that which is needed.

You must understand that you cannot take a life if you are a murderer and be allowed to live ordinarily again. Similarly when you seek release through suicide it means you have to live through that situation again.

In accidents there are always some that are unplanned (this is qualified by fact that they are people who have been the victim of a fast driver or someone who had not originally chosen to be a murderer but took that route because it gave a short term boost to their value), and they may end a life. That person must then relive their life so that they can reach the level of ability and worth needed.

Murder is not always pre-planned although some is. So the need always shows for some players to relive their lives and bring changes necessary to their progress. They must make recompense otherwise they may not achieve the necessary level of fulfilment given by God to those who are worthwhile. It is not always necessary to pause this need to create worth without generating goodness within.

And that cannot happen without generating good within that will reshape the values that surround you. For the giving of love is bound to commit everyone to generate worth, no matter how small.

You must understand that God provides what everyone needs so that they have the formula needed to serve their lives.

The Writing

The living of a life must be purposeful. And if it is without purpose it will end. For the purpose will not be there to maintain a need for it.

If it is given that a person shall live a long life of worth, and it transcends to a greater level of worth than was anticipated, it shall be that they shall live until that time of worth is ended, and they have concluded a need no more to stay.

But that giving of power to withstand pain and upset sometimes means that a person can live within a space of say, six months a need to generate not fear but an abundance of worth; so that they may qualify for a better level of worth within the realms of spirit. For they have formulated a better way forward and the learning of pain and of upset has brought them a need to generate valour. For that has given them an ability to combat illness within the mind, and it has given them a need to generate more time within their lives, so that they may live more and be more successful in their learning.

Let it be that some do not know how long they may live until the need shows for it. It can be that they are derelict in a need to serve God, and it has not been brought to them yet that they are to serve. And so they are able to live a long and healthy life until the need shows for some to be otherwise.

For they, who have not formulated the need to succeed within a special time can reawaken their spirits with a need to generate worth and find God in the meantime; so that they are awakened both to the call of God's need to serve, but also to a need to serve their own generation of power within the world.

Accidents and Suicides: Suicide is not pre-planned and it is not to be recommended as a way out of a framework of a life that is full of upset, for a suicide can bring only temporary change to the person who has ended their life. And they must relive that which they have avoided so that they may overcome that which is needed to be repelled in life.

Let it be now that you understand that you cannot take a life, if you are a murderer and be allowed to live ordinarily again. And it is the same in suicide whereby you seek release from what is an upsetting situation of some magnification, and it cannot bring release but a need to relive the situation.

In accidents there are always some that are unplanned and they may end a life. So that person must relive if they are unable to complete their life and bring forth that which is of ability and worth in their lives.

It is necessary to say here that the accidents I refer to are those where one has been the errant victim of a fast driver, or one who has not willed themselves to be a murderer but has chosen to take a life because it has been worthwhile to them not to move forward, but give a short term value to their life.

Murder is not always pre-planned although some is so that the need shows for the players of some roles to relive their lives and bring the changes necessary that they may move on. For they may not achieve that level of fulfilment necessary that God gives out to all who achieve worth.

It is necessary not always to forestall a need to generate worth, but it is of need sometimes. And that cannot be without a need to generate a goodness within that shall shape the worths of all around you.

For that of the giving of love shall place in all people a need to generate worth no matter how small.

Let it be that you understand that God's provision is to be of substance to all people, and to bring to them a need to live so that the application of such worths necessary shall bring them a need to serve."

Your Life (Channelled 15 May 2007)

Key Points

- Living to the full means reaching our full potential.
- God gives us what is in our hearts but we choose whether to be good or evil.
- The soul needs to experience good and bad.
- God's love awakens the need for good, so that there is more good than bad in the world.
- There must be a justice system.
- We choose what is right for us. We cannot choose wrongly. We have to reason fully beforehand.
- We are given the freedom to choose our way of progressing, but it must satisfy God's Principles which govern our achievement or failure.
- God will support each individual through his or her choice.
- Angels, fairies and those who have been absolved of their sins ensure that good will prevail at all times.

- There is a need for bad in the world. One type brings a short term effect, but the second accumulates and lasts with the purpose of overcoming good.
- When needed, Brother Satan brings evil to the world. He was brought to cause upset so that a final account must be met.
- The Devil does not harm people; he fuels their ability to be bad. But to whatever degree they achieve it, the White Light Of God overcomes all evil.

A Clear Account

In this, Jesus says that it is good to live life fully so that we achieve our full potential.

God gives us what is in our hearts whether we choose good or evil, but we can only choose evil if it is to be part of our work. We need an equal and opposing force in our lives so that we can learn. That may involve being partly bad. God's Love fulfils a purpose and it must be seen for what it is – a soul's need to experience evil and to have a need to be bad.

God's love can only deliver that which serves God's Awakening, His Power. Where there is an upset in the world there must be a larger force of good, and there must be a justice system to bring about changes. Goodness must win where there is a justice system in place.

We cannot choose anything that is not right for us. In a previous life, we may have been powerful, and it would not be right to wield the same amount of power again. God allows us to choose so that we can progress but we must satisfy His principles and win or fail accordingly.

There must be sound reasoning in the choice, but God then supports each person in whatever they choose. Good must prevail so there are angels, fairies and spirits who have been given absolution to ensure this force is present.

You must understand that good prevails because it needs to, but there is also a strong need for bad in the world. That can manifest in different ways. There is bad that passes quickly, and there is the sort that accumulates in an attempt to overcome good. It cannot tell between the good of God and that of the people so it is defeated when God's Power is brought against it.

Brother Satan steps in when a Devil's approach is needed. He does not bring evil to the world so that he can worship it, but so that the level of upset ensures that a final account must be met by the individuals involved.

You must understand that the Devil does not bring harm to people, but he fuels their ability to be bad to whatever degree they need including demonic powers. However it all has to end when God calls for it, and the White Light Of God will overcome all evil so that good prevails.

The Writing

It is good to live in full, because that brings the potential we feel to the full, and that can bring an astonishing amount of energy to its fulfilment.

For that which we hold in our hearts is given by God and that can be good or evil according to our choice. And that need to be of evil approach can only be accommodated if we are truly to serve the need in the fulfilment of our work.

For we are not evil by purpose. It is a need to bring an equal and opposing force to our lives that gives us the opportunity to learn by being evil. And that may not bring an evil; approach in full, but a partial one.

For the giving of God's Love is to serve in a fulfilment of a purpose. And that must be see for what it is, for it is the fulfilment of a soul's needs to experience that which is of evil approach and bring a need to be bad.

For that of the giving of God's Love can bring only that destined to be of service to God's awakening. And that need to substitute good for evil is a way of evening up the upset of the world so there is more that is good than there is evil. And also there needs to be a justice system that brings about changes in our lives.

For we are surrounded by bad characters and evil worth, but that may not govern where there is a goodness felt. For the goodness must win where there is a justice system for good to prevail.

It is good to know when we make our choice that we cannot choose that which is wrong for us. For we have

been of abounding faith until the time of choosing our
career in this life, and then it must be that we choose
our need to follow on.

For it may be that we have asserted our strength in
a previous life, and it would not be right if we generated
too much power in a later one. For we are formulated as
we formulate, and that must bring discernment to the
character so that we choose well.

It is God's approach to leave us to choose our will's
need to move on, and then to follow that with a need
to satisfy God's principles whether they are to fail or
to win.

For the formula to work fully there must be an accurate reasoning of the worth of the person, so they may
choose to be good or bad through reasoning and not
through a foolish act. But it is God's principle to support
that person through his or her choice and that will be
paramount. If the good force is weaker it will not prevail and that cannot be, so there is an accumulation of
good held in the worth of angels and fairies and those
who have passed before and been given absolution for
their sins. For they are of true character to good and
that must prevail at all times.

Let it be that you understand now a need to realise
that good prevails because there is a need to. But there
is also a powerful need to supply bad in a world where
all is not to be good. And that can be brought in many
ways, and it may constitute a freedom to live that emu-
lates bad but is not really bad.

But it is given a need somehow to serve as a frolic, as a general way of upset that will not prolong but will give out within a short time.

And then there is a prevailing bad that shall come and accumulate as the world carries on, and that must be given serious consideration, as it will be there to defeat good if it can.

But it is not able to discern between the goodness of God and that of the people, so it is brought to its knees when that of God's power is brought against it.

When there is a Devil's approach needed, it is given to our Brother Satan who is bringer of all evil to the world. And he was brought to the world not to encounter problems and worship them, but to bring the wrath of upset so that a final account must be met.

Let it be that you understand now that the Devil brings not harm to people, but upset in a way that fuels their capacity to be bad.

And that magnification can give a person demonic powers if they wish it. And it can bring upset like no one has yet known. But it must all end at the calling of God.

For that which is attributed to the White Light of God shall overcome all evil and good shall prevail.

Your Mindset
(Channelled 16 May 2007)

Key Points

- It is easy to warn about negativity but you may be negative anyway.
- It is best to be positive and value what you do.
- Unfortunately there has to be some conflict and only your mindset makes it a positive or negative experience.
- We are made that way, so attitude rules.
- Being eloquent and educated brings advantages to your progress.
- If necessary you can change direction and concentrate on a truer pathway of good.
- You can choose, but select the way that offers a kinder and simpler direction.

A Clear Account

It would be easy to start with warnings about being negative, but if you tend to think negatively it is likely you will be anyway.

It is best in fact to be positive and make things you do special. That way you avoid things going wrong.

Unfortunately this does not happen for there is bound to be some conflict and only your mindset can turn it from an upsetting experience to a positive one.

For that is how we are formulated, and so it is our attitude that will have its day.

Say you are eloquent and well spoken and all you have is that need to move forward. It is good to work out a way to be wise and worthwhile, but if this is not possible you can change direction and care less about the qualities you possess and instead concentrate on a truer pathway of good.

It is up to you which direction you take, but just take the one that offers a kinder and more willing route.

The Writing

It is possible to begin this with forebodings about negative thinking, but if you generate enough of a thought process that it can be negative, it is likely you will have the attitude of a negative person anyway.

For the need now recommends that we think pleasant thoughts and do special things if we are to avoid the panic of upset.

Unfortunately it is not true, for the way forward cannot be free of conflict, and it is only your mindset that can change the flow of energy from upset to a well mind. For that is how we are set and if that is to be the case, it is attitude that will have its day.

Let it be that you are eloquent and well spoken and that need to generate forth is all you possess.

It is good if you formulate a process by which you will become wise and worthwhile, but if this is not possible you can change tack and become a person who cares less about the worths held unto you and concentrate more on generating a new and truer pathway of obligation to good.

Let it be that you do not have to resort to this pattern but are able instead to give your all to a kinder more willing stance.

Z

Zest and Vigour
(Channelled 24 May 2007)

Key Points

- Some people lack zest and vigour because they do not exercise enough.
- The need for exercise can bring about grumpiness and upset people.
- Nowadays we tend to worship food and the effect of this can be upset stomachs and intestines, leading to aggressive behaviour and sometimes a shortening of life.
- Fatty and sugary foods upset our systems, and some drinks do.
- Allow more time to digest food and do not snack.
- Eat pulses, organic vegetables and similar foods and you will feel the energy return.
- Exercise and eat properly and it will help weight to fall and energy to rise fully.

A Clear Account

Jesus states here that zest and vigour is lacking in some people's lives because they do not take enough exercise. In all areas of life this is essential but it can make people grumpy and upset. He reminds us that we do not serve God by only looking after our minds and spirits we also have to care for our bodies.

Nowadays we tend to worship food and it is not a healthy thing to do, because it upsets our stomachs and intestines and as a result we can behave badly and our life expectancy can be affected.

People need to stay well and they cannot do this by eating too much or drinking in a way that affects the stomach. They should be wiser. They should be generous but not irresponsible in the way they eat and drink, otherwise they will pay the price. So much time is spent creating and eating fatty and sugary foods and these upset the system.

You should allow yourself more time to digest food and it is best not to snack too much. If you do this you will achieve a better quality of life.

Also be selective about the foods you eat, because changing your eating habits can increase your stamina and your mental alertness. You are not generally aware that you are performing less well in your work, but if you eat pulses, organic vegetables and other similar foods you will notice the energy return. And do not ignore the need for exercise for it helps the weight to fall and the energy to rise fully.

The Writing

It is now needed to talk about the zest and vigour that some people lack because they do not do enough exercise. It is necessary in all walks of life to exercise, and that need can bring about grumpiness and an upset behaviour.

For the worship of God is not only by looking after our minds and spirits, but also to look after our bodies, for we are not able to resist the worship of food nowadays and it is not healthy to do this for we are upsetting the behaviour of our stomachs and intestines also. And that can lead to aggressive behaviour and upset of types that can affect our life expectancy.

For the need of man is to stay healthy and he can do neither by allowing the need to eat too much or to drink also that which upsets the stomach. He is needed to be wise and able to support that need to be generous but not flagrant, and he must eventually pay the price if he is unable to address the issue. For the need for man to eat too much is an evident result of all the time spent eating and creating foods that are fatty and sugary and upsetting to the system.

Let it be soon that you allow yourself more time to digest between meals and do not snack so much, for it is willingness to address this that will give you a better life; and a willingness to hold within that need to be selective about meals. For the rearrangement of your habits can increase your stamina and your mental alert-

ness. For you are not aware when you are not performing fully in the need to work and be active, but if you
are given a full meal of bio* prepared vegetables and
also pulses and other similar items you can feel the energy return. And it is not necessary to relinquish the
need to exercise, but it helps the weight to fall and the
energy to rise fully.

**An explanation of bio prepared vegetables: I mean those
that are grown in organic conditions and not those that are
chemically protected and fertilised.*

The Last Word
(Channelled 12 May 2007)

It is good to be aware of everything in your life; all that influences you that is good and that which is bad for you.

It is influence that governs our lives if we allow it, and yet it is your pathway and your way forward, that is important. So you must always influence your own decisions by making yourself aware of all that is about you.

Let it be that you are gaining experience as a factory worker. Maybe it is a good job and maybe not for you, but you are aware of everything about you as you contemplate the decision, and gain the capability to choose between that and another job.

For you are wakening to a need now to bring to your life a better fabric, a need to generate a better loyalty to yourself, so it serves you better and awakens your desire for more of the same.

You are arriving at a decision now. You have decided to view this book and arrive at a decision whether to buy it. If it is a good book, you will want it and if it is not, it will stay on the shelf. But it is the accumulation of such knowledge that makes you aware, and gives you the ability to choose.

So be aware and take the challenge that this book offers you. For it will bring your knowledge to another level. And it will bring within you a need to contemplate what is better for the soul, and not just what is better for the mind and the body.

For it is the soul that brings you your life, and it is your soul's pathway that will benefit if you choose well. So choose and be well in your choice. For you are God's Child and I will reawaken in you a need to serve the Pathway of God through fulfilment and not misery. I will be there for you at every turn, and in every paradigm, there will be a coming of events that says that this shall be the time when I am aware of the Lord's Presence.

For the coming of my need to serve has been as a result of that written by Frances Munro. For she has been my channelling force in this book and she has brought a need to serve in all abilities to be of service unto God. And that will be through the channelling of my wisdom to the way forth.

Let it be that you need to serve God, and that you buy this book, for it will bring you a capability beyond imagination to enjoy and endure through all walks of life and beyond, in the happiness needed to be of service to God's values.

Let it be soon that you learn God's values to be of service to yourself. And I will be with you at all times, for you to be strong and worthwhile in all that you do.

I am the Christ and I will serve you and fulfil you in all ways, to serve the values of God in His Name, and I will be with you through and through in my name of Jesus.

ISBN 142513882-9

9 781425 138820